Hills of Home

DEBBIE RICHARD

eLectio Publishing, LLC
Little Elm, TX
www.eLectioPublishing.com

Hills of Home
By Debbie Richard

Cover Design by eLectio Publishing, LLC

ISBN-13: 978-1-63213-021-1
Published by eLectio Publishing, LLC
Little Elm, Texas
http://www.eLectioPublishing.com

Printed in the United States of America

Publisher's Note

In loving memory of my mother, Naomi Karen Richard

July 12, 1936 – March 7, 2011

And my father, Arlis Dewain Richard

July 15, 1933 – April 18, 1983

Table of Contents

Acknowledgments

Grateful acknowledgments to:

My late mother, Naomi Karen Richard, for her superb storytelling, and for her love and support which have been invaluable;

My aunts, Lyla Kopshina and Louise Mathess Dewees, who provided me with a glimpse into their childhood;

Carrie McCullough of McCullough Consulting, for her careful reading of this book and for invaluable editing and guidance;

South Carolina Writers' Workshop and West Virginia Writers, Inc., and to the members I have met through these fine organizations;

Sherry Hardee, for always believing in me;

Cheryl and Shirley Atkinson, for their friendship and encouragement;

Doris Skipper, who has been like a second mother;

And to my dear friend Janet (Walker) Murphy, who has been such an inspiration for this book.

Preface

I began writing *Hills of Home* while full-time caregiver for my mother in March 2009, and with her help, descriptive stories of growing up in rural Calhoun County, West Virginia, and many photographs of family and places in the Mountain State, my manuscript was completed in 2010.

I'm grateful for my mother's storytelling ability and the precious time we had together working on this manuscript. Sadly, she along with my Uncles Denzil Richard and Joe Kopshina, and West Virginia Poet Laureate, Irene McKinney passed away before *Hills of Home* was published. In tribute and loving memory to them, I have left the manuscript as it was before their passing. Evidence of this will appear in later sections of the book.

I can relate with the late Irene McKinney who shared in an interview, *"I want very much to work against the stereotype that living in the mountains, living in Appalachia is some kind of paradise on earth. We all know that isn't true. It's rough. These choices are rough. A lot of isolation, a lot of limited job opportunity....a lot of being cut off from the larger world at times. It's equally as important to look at that....as the positive side. The positive side is nothing without that underlayment of the gritty parts of life..."*

I was born and raised in West Virginia, as were both my parents. Currently living near the beautiful South Carolina coastline, I am a far distance from West Virginia geographically speaking, but my heart and memories, always have been, and always will be, in the "hills of home."

Introduction

The hills of West Virginia often call me, even though I live over five hundred miles away now, in a world so fast-paced I can hardly catch my breath.

When people think of West Virginia, hillbillies with corncob pipes, mountain feuds, and moonshiners often come to mind – not so in my family.

In my early years, we lived in the remote, rural community of Munday, West Virginia, in Wirt County. We lived beside my Grandma Richard and Uncle Denzil with only a few shade trees between property lines. We explored the tall hills behind our house and across the road in front of us. There were plenty of trees, but the woods back then were not thick with underbrush. We had a large front yard that went down to the creek and a footbridge crossed it. The main road, which was paved, was not wide enough to need a yellow line down the center. The local folks knew to slow down when they happened to meet another car, and to take it easy around a curve.

Times were simpler. We went to a little, two-room school about a mile from home. We played games at recess like Hide and Seek or Red Rover, Red Rover. There weren't drugs or weapons to evoke fear in us. My aunt cooked the meals for the school, and our teachers really cared that we learned—not only our lessons from books, but lessons from life—the importance of getting along, and having respect for one another and our parents.

A few years later, when my dad relocated us because of his job, we moved near the little town Walton, West Virginia. There, I met a kindred spirit, my dear friend, Janet. I found out what it was like to have a life-long friend, one you could share your deepest thoughts. We spent many lovely afternoons roaming the hills together, picking wildflowers, or wading through the creek.

I didn't know at the time that we didn't have much as the world might measure, but when I see children today, as young as kindergarteners, sitting in front of computers, my heart is filled with sadness that they'll never experience life as I did. They've never had the pleasure of giving their dolls a bath in the creek or hanging their clothes on their mother's clothesline. They've never walked the country road to the store to buy a bottle of soda pop on a hot summer's day, or walked the hills and hollows and seen the Jack-in-the-Pulpits or the yellow Lady Slippers blooming, or picked Trilliums and the purple Sweet Williams for their mothers. They've never experienced what it's like to have known the "hill ways" of home remedies, and helping neighbors who are in need. Even when times were hard and we veered off the path from which we were raised, there was hope we'd get back on track.

These stories are memories that I cherish from my earliest childhood when I lived near my Grandma Richard to the time I became an adult. Not everyone has had close-knit family ties and childhood friendships which have spanned a lifetime. My desire is these stories will enlighten those less fortunate who've not had the pleasure of living a rural country life in the hills and to embrace the memories of those who have.

Chapter 1
A Time to Cherish

Hideaway

The dirt laid beneath me, cool, inviting, as I rested my young body flush against the earth. A grownup might be less likely to brave the unknown.

It was cooler under the house in the summer, and since Dad hadn't had a chance to put the shiny, metal underpinning on the house yet, it was easy access for me. Mom got down on her hands and knees and peered under the house, and to her relief, discovered I was sleeping peacefully in the darkness and coolness of my favorite hideaway.

She tugged on my dress and called to me, softly, as not to startle me. I roused, stretched, and slowly opened my eyes to find her reaching for me.

They were having a celebration next door at Grandma Richard's house, and we were already late. Today was Grandpa Pepper's birthday. His full name was Robert Omer Pepper, but the family just called him Grandpa. He was Grandma Edna Richard's dad. The family met at Grandma's once a year to celebrate his birthday. They were so scattered that they didn't get a chance to all get together very often, but when they did, what a celebration. Everyone brought food from miles around – fried chicken, potato salad, those big, three-layer chocolate cakes and coconut cream pies, to name a few. They ate and visited for hours, reminiscing and catching up on all the news. Their lively chatter filled the house, and spilled out into the yard.

Uncle Basil and Aunt Audrey came from Ohio, as did Uncle Denward and Aunt Nina. Aunt Ethel and Uncle Ralph came from Elizabeth, West

Virginia, and Uncle Abner ("Ab" as he was known) from Munday. Edna's youngest daughter, Lyla, came with her husband, Joe, and their young son, Jimmy, from Nutter Fort, which is just on the outskirts of Clarksburg, West Virginia.

Some sat in the yard under large shade trees, some sat on the back porch, or on the wide banisters of the front porch, drinking in the fragrance of the nearby lilac bush; some sat on the cool cement steps out front under the large shade tree – also a nice place to watch the local traffic go by – waving to friends and neighbors who passed.

Mom took me in the house, cleaned me up, dressed me in my red-and-white dress with little canvas shoes to match. She brushed my blond curls until they shone, and then we joined the rest of the family. My dad was already there. He swooped me up in his arms when he saw me. I was bashful and he knew just how I felt. He, too, was uncomfortable in crowds. My dad, Arlis, was Edna's youngest child, and she was pleased when he decided to build our house on the property adjoining hers because she would always have family nearby. (We lived in Parkersburg when I was born. While there, Dad worked at a chemical plant for a while and then drove a delivery truck for a bread company, but he soon returned to the hills where he was raised and where he wanted his children to grow up).

Dad carried me around with him for a while, long enough to visit with some of the relatives. We soon crept away from the crowd, however, walking back over to our house where he made me a peanut butter sandwich. Perching me on his shoulders, we walked down through the bottom, past the vegetable garden, and down to the creek where we sat and listened to the water as it washed peacefully over the rocks.

Aunt Ellen's

I must have been about three at the time of Grandpa Pepper's celebration when my dad carried me away from the crowd, but about a year earlier, we lived in the same community near Aunt Ellen. She and Grandpa Richard were brothers and sisters.

In the wintertime, Mom dressed me in my warm clothes and little white boots and we walked together down the path to Aunt Ellen's, often in the snow. She lived in a two-story, older house with no paint on it. I remember it being tall and gray. But the inside was warm and inviting. Aunt Ellen looked forward to our visits. We visited in the sitting room. The white doilies which topped the end tables in that room were made with delicate stitching, not unlike many of my mother's. A vase of flowers or a family Bible also adorned these. Adjoining the sitting room was the dining room, and I can still remember a chocolate layer cake sitting on the table in that room. The bitter taste of the dark chocolate was different than anything I had tasted before.

We only lived in the little house near Aunt Ellen for a short while, until Mildred insisted we move out so her son, Tom, and his wife, Carolyn, could have it. Mildred just lived up the creek a little ways, and now she would have her son and daughter-in-law living near her.

We had to move in with Grandma Richard until Dad got our house built next to hers. Of course, I didn't mind this arrangement at all, for Grandma and I were very close. Dad, along with Orlan Wilson and some of the other neighbors, built our house partly from the lumber Dad retrieved when he tore down Grandma's old barn. They used tarpaper shingles to cover the outside of the house, and put a tin roof on it. They built a porch that led into the kitchen. Later, Dad put the shiny underpinning on for the skirting.

His Uncle Roy taught him how to build, as he had helped him build Kenneth and Phyllis Munday's house near the little Methodist Church. Uncle Roy and Okey Richard, dad's dad, were brothers. I never met my grandfather, who passed away when my dad was a teenager.

Playing in the Potato Patch

When I was small, about three or four years old, Mom would get me all cleaned up and I would go down to Grandma's potato patch after a rain, and sit in the holes where the potatoes had been dug out. Grandma's garden was in sight of our house and not as far away as our big potato patch, which covered a whole field of land. She shared the new potatoes with us, and we used to "gravel" them out with a fork, taking care not to bruise the tender skins. I suppose I thought I was helping out, and I was having such fun playing in the tiny mud holes.

Those first new potatoes made the best "boiled and fried potatoes" as Mom called them. She washed the potatoes, but didn't peel the skins off; then, she would boil them until tender, drain them and put them in a skillet of bacon drippings to brown. How wonderful they tasted!

New potatoes made good potato salad, too. She often made that along with homemade baked beans and fried chicken to take on a picnic when we went to watch Dad play softball with the other men. Teams were formed when some of the men in the local neighborhood got together. They played against such teams as Elizabeth, MacFarlan or Harrisville. I still have a photograph of us at one of his games.

My help with the potatoes and other farming was not without problems for Mom. I'd probably go through three or four sets of clothes in a day. And back then, wash day was no easy chore. Mom had to wash our clothes on a ringer washing machine, rinse them in a big aluminum tub, and then run them through the ringer again to get the excess water out. They would have to be hung on the clothesline to dry, and then they were ready for ironing the next day. Oh, the love and patience of a mother!

The Outhouse

When we were growing up, and before indoor plumbing, we had an outhouse which we shared with Grandma Richard and her son, Denzil. Uncle Denzil worked in the oil fields and lived at home, as he never married. The outhouse was not located conveniently in our backyard, but on the other side of Grandma's house, past her tall rose of Sharon bush with its pink blossoms, which was more like a tree as it had grown so tall, and past her garden, bordered with the lovely cornflower-blue morning glories that greeted each day. Grandma would often notice my mom as she passed by on the way to the outhouse and I would be hurrying behind her, my blond curls bouncing in the wind.

"Karen, she won't let you out of her sight," Grandma would comment with a chuckle.

At night, after dark, we used a chamber pot. It was made of porcelain, like the old fashioned white dishpans. The pot had a lid and a wire bail to carry it with. We had to be careful not to spill it during the night, and we emptied it in the outhouse the next morning.

One particular visit to the outhouse was memorable. I opened the door and stepped inside, sat down on the wide, wooden seat when I happened to look up and see a long black snake observing me from the ledge above the door. I'm not sure which of us was the most startled, but I would imagine that was the shortest visit to the outhouse I had experienced. I was up and out of there in a flash!

We didn't have indoor plumbing until I was about eight years old when Dad built a room onto our back porch. The bathroom had a hot water tank, a shower, and a commode, great luxuries for a house. The ringer washing machine was also in there. Before that, bathing was more cumbersome. We drew water from the well and heated it in a dishpan on the stove in the utility room (the gas stove in the utility room was also used for canning); then we poured the water in a round galvanized tub to take a bath.

Aunt Louise, my dad's sister, shared a story about growing up with outdoor plumbing. While she was living at home, her boyfriend Jack Mathess and some of his buddies came by one day. Mischievous as they were, they decided to play a prank on Asa. When he went to the outhouse, Jack and the other boys followed him and turned the outhouse over. There was Asa - just sitting on the wooden seat for the whole world to see. It gave a new meaning to the word "out" house!

Mud Pies

Jack Mathess lived at Hartley, out the ridge from what is now known as Brohard, after some of the family by the same name, and not too far from where my Aunt Louise grew up at Munday. When he and Aunt Louise married, they moved to Ohio. My dad went to stay with them for a while and found a job there. This was after Dad had graduated from high school and before he and Mom married, and before he was drafted into the Army. Jack and Louise had a daughter, Sheila. When Sheila was a little girl, she wanted to make pies and asked her Uncle Arlis if he would crack some black walnuts for her. He worked painstakingly on the task, as black walnuts are very hard to crack, and even harder to pick out the little kernels from their shells. Once he had gotten what he thought would be enough for pie baking, he gave them to her and went on about his business. Later that day, he came upon her playing in the yard, and much to his dismay, he saw the home she had found for the walnuts – they were nestled in her pile of mud pies!

Courtship

My dad, the youngest of five children, grew up in the little community of Munday, West Virginia, in Wirt County and my mom grew up near Industry in Calhoun County, about five miles away. They met at a revival meeting at the United Brethren Church where Mom and her family attended. They started seeing each other when they were in their teens.

I've seen pictures of my dad when he was a teenager, and I thought he was handsome. But, don't all little girls think that of their daddy? In his high school senior picture, he didn't look that much different than he did when he was six years old; a little taller and wiser maybe, but he still had that same boyish smile, brown hair that was parted on the side, and blue eyes a girl could swim in. Mom was beautiful, at least I thought so. She had blue eyes and dark brown hair she kept curled and brushed back at the temples. When Mom was a little girl, she had pale blond hair, just like mine.

Dad was drafted into the Army, and he did his basic training at Fort Campbell, Kentucky, before he was shipped overseas to Japan. He and Mom got married while he was home on leave. Rev. J. M. Snider married them at his home in Freed, West Virginia, with Rev. Snider's wife, Ola Snider, and Dad's Mom, Edna Richard, in attendance.

My oldest brother Joe was born in Grantsville in Calhoun County while Dad was still in the service. Joe was born on Mother's Day. He was a whopping baby boy weighing in at ten pounds and five-and-a-half ounces. He was a beautiful baby, if you can call boys beautiful. Mom and Joe lived with Grandma Maze while Dad was away, and everybody doted on little Joey. They told Mom there was snow on the roof of The Bowling Clinic when he was born, and it was very unusual to see snow in May, even in the hills.

Swaying Christmas Tree

One Christmas while Dad was in the Army, Uncle Jack and Aunt Louise came to celebrate at Grandma Richard's house. Mom was there with Joe, who was just a toddler. Joe had a favorite box he had been playing with at our grandmother's house. Of course, Uncle Jack wasn't aware of this when he decided to use that same box to set the Christmas tree on to make it a little taller. While their backs were turned, Joe crawled under the tree and tried to retrieve his toy. When they glanced back around, they found the tree swaying as if in a wind storm. Obviously, they had to find another solution to raise their Christmas tree.

Pickled "Tinky" Corn

During a conversation about growing up in the hills, Mom remembered a particular canning season when I was about two years old and my older brother was about six.

We had a cellar made of cement blocks. They made the cellar by cutting out the side of a hill and placing cement blocks in there to make a cool place to store home-canned vegetables and the like, as well as potatoes, onions and apples through the winter. Cement was poured for the floor of the cellar and a door was put on the front. A large room was built overhead for storage.

Mom would take a five-gallon, stone jar, fill it full of ears of corn and make a salt brine to pour over it so it would sour or pickle. She placed a dinner plate upside down over the ears of corn as a weight, and then put a clean white cloth over the jar and tied it securely with twine. She let it set for three or four weeks in the cellar. We could hardly wait until the pickled corn was ready. One time, while I was eating it, with the salt brine running down my face, I reached for another ear of corn and said, "Joe, give me another ear of that tinky corn." My family thought that was amusing, and from that day forward they referred to it as "tinky" corn.

Farming and Other Chores

When my brother, Joe, was about ten years old, we had a big corn patch beyond Grandma Richard's house. Joe didn't like working in the corn field. He complained it was too hot and that hoeing made his back hurt. I would have been about six at the time, and helped hoe corn right along with the rest. Mom didn't remember me complaining much when it came to helping out.

She glanced around at Joe once, and there he was – barefoot, with his blue jeans rolled up, his white t-shirt, and that crew cut Dad and the boys were wearing – down on his hands and knees in the dirt, hoeing (if you could call it that), hoping somebody would feel sorry for him. With the sun beating down on his head, he was probably thinking of all the other things he'd rather be doing – riding his bicycle, fishing, or wading in the cool creek below the house – anything but the chore at hand. Dad always said Joe didn't think much of farming.

Joe complained about washing dishes when he was in his early teens, whining that his hands were all withered and he had "dishpan hands" from doing "woman's work." My younger brother, Jay, however, didn't suffer with the "dishpan hands" syndrome. When he was six years old, he would put Mom's striped apron on and pull a little white chair over so he could reach the sink. He actually wanted to wash dishes. I have a picture of him standing on that little chair, smiling for the camera, washing dishes, with a whole stack of dirty ones piled high on the sink beside him.

First Day of School

A few years passed and it was the first day of school – a scary time for a little girl who has held so tight to her mom's dress tail.

My first school was Bell School, a two-room schoolhouse in our little community. The school taught grades first through sixth. My first teacher was Mrs. Henrietta Mills. Mrs. Mills had short, light brown hair – either naturally curly, or with the help of a permanent wave, and she wore glasses. She was of slender build and had a pleasant demeanor.

On the first day of school, I picked out a seat and started to sit down, when to my amazement a little girl said to me, "You've taken my seat." I found another seat. I couldn't imagine a seat already reserved on the first day of school. Nor did I know then that Elaine Toney would become one of my close friends in the days and years that followed.

Our school was in the country, and had two rooms which were divided by folding doors. This allowed Mrs. Mills to teach the younger grades on one side and Mrs. Cora Quick to teach the older grades on the other. Mrs. Quick had dark, wavy hair, brushed back at the temples and flipped up slightly in the back. She wore dark-rimmed glasses. She appeared rather stern when she wasn't smiling, but when she smiled her features took on a softer expression.

There was a large chalkboard at the front of the class in each room. Ours was black with the letters of the alphabet printed just above it in both capital and small letters. The chalkboard in Mrs. Quick's room was on either side of the doorway and it was green. Above the doorway was a poster of the American flag. A poster of Abraham Lincoln hung over the chalkboard on the left of the door, and a poster of George Washington hung on the right. Both rooms had wooden floors. Bookshelves were neatly arranged around the room. Windows were partitioned with several panes which captured our attention, especially on snowy days in the winter and in the springtime as sunshine streamed in, warming us and promising the awakening of wild flowers.

Recess

Recess was always a favorite time at Bell School. We played outside on pretty days, carefree games such as: A Tisket, A Tasket (Drop the Hanky), London Bridge, Red Rover-Red Rover, Hide and Seek or Hopscotch on the covered, cement porch.

When the weather wasn't as favorable, we played games inside such as Jacks or we might draw on an Etch-a-Sketch. I brought my Etch-a-Sketch to school one day when one of the Metz boys took it away from me. I wanted it back, and told Mrs. Quick what had happened. With a deep frown on her face, she pulled the black, leather paddle from her top desk drawer, and took him out in the hall and gave him a whippin'. The paddle was fierce looking and cut full of holes. We were terrified of it. I remember how awful I felt hearing that paddle hit his backside. Swat! Swat! Swat!

That taught me a lesson that day, too; not only did he have to pay the consequences for what he had done, but I had to live with myself for telling on him.

Some of my friends I remember from Bell School were Tom and Carolyn Pettit's daughter, Roberta or "Bertie," Lewis and Sue Pettit's daughter, Lou Ann, Kenneth and Phyllis Munday's daughter, Pam, who lived just out the lane – on the other side of the Methodist church, the Bunner children from down the road – between our house and the school, and the Metz children from up at Brohard, about five or six miles away. Steve Simmons lived a few houses above Grandma Richard's; Elaine Toney lived on the hill above the store; Sherry Rose, and her sister, Debbie, lived on the Munday road toward Grantsville, and Barbara Frye. I still have group pictures of my classmates from 1965, 1967 and 1968; I treasure these.

Lunch Time

Lunches for the entire school were prepared by my Aunt Faye Munday, and were they delicious! There was a drop-down window on one side of Mrs. Mills' classroom that led into the kitchen where Aunt Faye did all the cooking. When she dropped the wooden partition down, we all lined up for lunch. I still remember big bowls of vegetable soup and chunks of her homemade cornbread.

Our little community of Munday was named after Aunt Faye's husband's family. I liked Uncle Virge Munday. He was a nice man, and was willing to help his neighbors in any way he could.

Mrs. Orpha Mae Underwood was a teacher's assistant at the school. She was our neighbor, and we passed their house on our way to school. We just knew her as Orpha Mae. She was a young woman with dark, wavy hair she wore down to her shoulders. She was married to Jim Underwood, and they had a son named Donnie. They lived right beside Uncle Ross Munday and Aunt Lyda. Uncle Ross and Uncle Virge were brothers.

Orpha Mae drew very well. One day at lunch, she drew a bird on the chalkboard. I watched in amazement, and asked how she could draw like that. She asked me, in a very gentle voice, “Can’t you draw like this by looking at a picture?” She was holding a picture of a bird in her hand and drawing a replica right before my eyes.

I believe Orpha Mae was the inspiration for the enjoyment I’ve found in drawing. I started drawing from pictures in my coloring books such as Bambi and Thumper, to Cinderella and her Prince Charming, to a steamboat on the river, to a fall scene of harvested fruit – which won a red ribbon at a local festival many years ago.

Snack Time

Snack time in the afternoon at the two-room school consisted of cheese and orange juice – commodity foods. We took turns serving. One child handed out glasses of orange juice while another passed out the thick chunks of cheese Aunt Faye sliced and placed on a plate. I suppose I was a little over anxious when it came my turn because I took a piece of cheese off the plate and handed it to the first student in the front row, thinking I was being helpful. I continued serving this way until my teacher noticed and reminded me to let each student pick out their own. I was used to Mom placing food on the table for us, and I thought I was being helpful. I continued with the plate of cheese, allowing each student to choose their own. It was velvety smooth, almost buttery tasting, and the orange juice was rich and fresh, unlike what you would find in a store. We didn't have cheese and orange juice often at home, and these were both nutritious and delicious.

Valentine's Party

Valentine's Day was always a special time at school – one of my favorite times of the year. There was excitement in the air as we decorated a large cardboard box with red tissue paper and cut hearts out of construction paper and glued those on the box. It was so pretty. It had a hole cut out in the top to drop valentines.

The old-fashioned valentines were my favorite. Most of them had pictures of boys and girls or puppies and kittens and came with little white envelopes. They would be considered vintage now. They were not the cartoon-type that you find in stores now; most of the new ones just fold over and don't even come with envelopes. We exchanged valentines, taking turns passing the cards out. We exchanged valentines with everyone in the class, and had a nice collection to take home with us. At our party, we could eat all the hotdogs and brownies we wanted on that day. Some of the mothers, including mine, helped by baking brownies and supervising the games.

Birthday Party at Pam's

When we were about nine or ten years old, Pam's mom held a birthday party for her at their house out the lane from the school and invited several of her classmates.

Pam Munday was a pretty girl with long, brown hair that she wore in two braids, and she had bangs across her forehead. She had a delightful smile, and was well liked by her classmates.

We played a game at her party where her mom hid a red pin cushion in the house, while we waited outside. When we came back into the house, I walked right up to the spot where it was hidden, behind a photograph, and the others thought that I peeked, but I had not. I'm still not sure to this day how that happened.

Her birthday cake was store-bought, and it was a beautiful creation of layers with white icing and pink trim. It was amazing to a little girl to see so many slices could be cut from just one birthday cake. Pam's party was the only birthday party I remember going to as a child. Most people baked at home. A store-bought cake was a treat, but I loved Mom's homemade cakes. She made birthdays special for my brothers and me. She baked German chocolate cakes from scratch with coconut pecan icing that she cooked on the stove. These were our favorite. We celebrated our birthdays as a family, but I don't remember ever having a party.

Bookworm

Pam was the school's bookworm. It seemed she always had her nose in a book, even during recess. I think Pam liked to read anything she could get her hands on. I wouldn't be surprised if Pam became a teacher herself, but I lost touch with her after we moved away from Munday.

I especially liked to read the Bobbsey Twins and Nancy Drew. I recently ran across a flower book that I had made when I was in the third grade. We were given pictures of various flowers to color, one flower per page. When I'd finished, I used purple construction paper to make a front and back cover for my book; our teacher punched holes in each page, and I tied a satin ribbon through the holes to secure it. On the front of my book, I drew three flowers and wrote *"My Flower Book, Deborah Richard, Grade 3, 1967."*

Pie Social

One Saturday night, we had a pie social at Bell School. The folding doors between the two classrooms were opened up for the social. Girls brought homemade pies or cakes hidden in pretty boxes and tied with ribbons. Much preparation went into this evening as the girls and their mothers worked hard to prepare an appealing package which would go to the highest bidder. My pie was bid on by a man I considered a tough-looking neighbor. The man won the bid, but my dad talked him in to letting his son eat with me instead – much to my relief, I might add.

The money raised at the social was used to help the school – to have indoor restrooms put in to replace the outhouse, for example. My dad was president of the PTA and was responsible for this – which made me feel very proud.

Chapter 2

Munday: Country Living at its Best

Slicky-Slide

We didn't have swing sets, slides, or monkey bars like modern-day play sets you might see in any number of backyards today, but we had our own homemade slide when we lived at Munday. Dad designed and built us a slide next to the shade tree, on the bank beside our house, which was to the left of our house, as you are facing the front. This was as close as a backyard as we had, because really, the hills were our backyard. We spent many happy days playing back there.

Our slide wasn't like the narrow plastic slides you might notice in play sets or at the park. Dad built a wooden frame about three feet wide and twelve feet long with wooden steps for us to climb up on; then he covered the frame with big sheets of tin. We rubbed wax paper over the tin to make it slick, just like we used on the steel runners of our sleds to go flying over the snowy hills in the wintertime.

A little further down the path from where Dad built our slide, there was a large tree with a strong limb reaching out over the path. He drilled some holes in a board and took some heavy rope and ran it through the holes, and then tied our new swing to the tree limb. We could enjoy our own swing, right there on the cool, shaded path.

Just beyond our slide, and where the hill begins to incline behind our house, there was a blanket of the prettiest tall, red flowers growing. Mom planted these on the bank back there, and every year the patch of flowers came back, taller and fuller than the year before.

Elderberry Picking Time

Uncle Jack and Aunt Louise were at Grandma Richard's one fall when the elderberries were ripe. The elderberry bushes, or shrubs, grew down near the creek. Uncle Jack picked several clusters of the berries and brought them up to Grandma's front steps, to sit in the shade. The berries were tiny, much smaller than raspberries or blackberries, and it is a tedious job to pick them off clusters, but it was worth it because they made the best jelly ever. They dropped the berries into a pan that was sitting on the cool cement steps. Just as they were finishing up, my younger brother Jay, who was about four or five at the time, came bounding up the steps. His foot caught the corner of the pan, and the tiny berries went spilling all over the front yard. Dad looked at Uncle Jack and said, "Well, Jack, now we're even. Remember the walnuts?"

They all burst out laughing, remembering how Jack's daughter, Sheila, had talked her Uncle Arlis into picking out the black walnuts for her mud pies, and now it was turn about.

The Pony

Dad bought a pony for us, and we named him Mr. Ed after the horse on the TV show. Our pony didn't look anything like that Mr. Ed. Ours was a shiny, chestnut brown with two white patches on his sides. It was the summer of 1967 when my little brother Jay was seven years old, before his first heart surgery later that fall.

We didn't have a place to keep the pony at our house, but Lula was kind enough to let us use her barn and pasture. Since she didn't live very far from us, just down the path, we could see him often. Dad would bring Mr. Ed up to our house, and let us ride him down through the bottom. At the time, I was nine and Joe had just turned thirteen. Jay was little, so Dad could pick him up and set him on the pony, but sometimes Dad would lead the pony over to Grandma Richard's tall front steps so we could climb up and practice mounting him.

I think Joe was afraid of Mr. Ed. One day, Joe had been over at Grandma Maze's visiting. When she brought him back home, he saw the pony was down in the bottom with Dad, and exclaimed, "There's that D_ _ _ pony!" Grandma Maze got tickled at Joe, as this was so out of character for him.

During one ride, Mr. Ed started kicking when my little brother was riding him, and bucked him off. Dad took a switch to the pony. He was afraid we would get hurt, so Dad sold Mr. Ed to a man who lived over at Palestine, just outside of Elizabeth, about fifteen miles away.

After we moved to Walton in Roane County, Uncle Denzil took Jay back to Munday to visit Grandma for a week in the summer in the early 1970s, and on the way, they went through Elizabeth and Palestine so Jay could catch a glimpse of Mr. Ed at his new home. Jay was pleased to see he was out in the pasture field and had grown into a fine-looking horse.

The Fur Trade

Why my dad wanted to raise Chinchillas for the fur trade was a mystery to me. He'd heard the fur from chinchillas was popular because of its extremely soft texture, and it was the most expensive to own. Perhaps the fur from these chinchillas would clothe well-to-do women as far away as

Chicago or New York City. Surely it wouldn't be for the women we knew, the women who lived in the remote regions of West Virginia.

I suppose it wasn't all that unusual for a boy who lived in the hills, or even a young man as my dad was, to want to become an entrepreneur if there was the slightest possibility that this venture might seriously change his financial future.

Dad had to order the chinchillas as they weren't like hamsters, and couldn't be found in a local pet store – not even in a town as big as Parkersburg. Chinchillas are slightly larger than ground squirrels, and belong to the family Chinchillidae. The animal is named after the Native American people of the Andes who wore its soft, dense fur.

Several things factor in the survival of chinchillas, one being the climate. Chinchillas typically fare better in cool temperatures, as they can have heat stroke if overheated. Our chinchillas were active during the night and liked to sleep during the day, so they didn't really like for us to disturb them in the daytime. They were very active and playful, and needed roomy cages for exercise. Dad enclosed our front porch, and set up cages for the chinchillas. I must have been about ten at the time, and didn't really know what to think of these furry little things on our front porch.

They ate a regular supply of loose hay and the hay-based pellets Dad ordered for them. With gentle handling from a young age, most chinchillas become quite tame and bond closely with their owners, although sometimes they don't like to be held or cuddled. Dad's chinchillas never did multiply, and he tired of the project after a while. When he saw the fur trade wasn't going anywhere, Dad realized the large chinchilla farm was not to be. He decided to give them away to someone who could enjoy them as pets, much to my relief. He gave them to Mom's sister, Aunt Betty, who had a house full of children. They cared for them for a while, but eventually afforded them their freedom, and that was the end of the fur trade business.

Images

Looking back now, if I had taken everything into account about the way others perceived me – even from an early age – I might have developed an inferiority complex.

Although I've been told I was a pretty baby, and I've seen photos from about the time I was two years of age and beyond, I don't remember seeing any baby pictures of me in photo albums, or even packed away in boxes. I asked my mom about it one day and reminded her that I'd seen tons of photos of my brother, Joe, their firstborn. So, if they had a camera then, why didn't they take pictures of me, just four years later? Did they not want pictures of me? With a hurt look in her eyes, Mom told me that Dad sold the camera. I realized how that must have hurt Mom – not to have any pictures of her only baby girl – taking my first step, or celebrating my first birthday, or my first Christmas.

I only remember one picture of me when I was less than two years old. It was taken at Grandma Richard's house. It's a picture of me and my cousin, Jimmy Kopshina, who was just a little boy. He was sitting beside me in a chair with his arm around me, and his little thumb was touching my chubby cheek. I had a frilly dress on, and he must have been wearing shorts because I could see his bare legs, and we were both barefooted.

When I was about ten years old, I remember standing on the front porch of Grandma Richard's house with one of my uncles. Getting ready to go inside, he looked down at me and said, "You're really fat, aren't you?" and laughed.

I can still remember that laugh; something eerie about it. He didn't say fat the way I would say the word. He said "faaaaaaat" drawing it out with much emphasis. That day has haunted me some forty years later. I've had my share of weight problems, up and down like a yo-yo at times, much like many other Americans I suppose, but it wasn't until I was finally a senior in high school that I had lost enough weight to wear the ever-coveted size 10 dress. I felt like a beauty queen in my white sleeveless dress on graduation night.

Perhaps there have been things in our lives that have caused embarrassment or disappointment to us at one time or another. I'm so thankful for the love of our Heavenly Father. He doesn't perceive us the way the world does; regardless of the way we look, or if we are outgoing or somewhat "backward" as we used to say in the hills, it doesn't make Him love us any less.

Conspiracy

While I was still attending Bell School, I wanted to have a sleepover with one of my friends. However, it was hard for me to decide which girl to invite, if only one. I was torn between Barbara and another little girl named Debbie. Barbara had long, dark brown hair and a mature build for her age; Debbie was shorter with light brown hair, and when she grinned, you just knew she had to be up to something. I liked them both very much. So, I decided to invite them both, much to my mom's disapproval. She thought I should just invite one at a time. Both girls accepted my invitation, and I was looking forward to a great time, but was I ever fooled!

Barbara and Debbie whispered and giggled behind my back. The girls walked down to the edge of the creek and stood by our footbridge, talking amongst themselves. The weather was warm, so it was pleasant to be outside.

They would have nothing to do with me – and at my house, of all places! What a change of character I saw in them. It was like having two strangers at my house, instead of two of my friends. Moms know best, and I should have listened to her advice. When we went back to school, they acted like nothing had happened. Oddly enough, we remained friends.

Shimer's General Store

My brothers and I walked down to the general store about a half mile away to buy candy. We could get a paper bag full of candy bars for a quarter and a bottle of (soda) pop for a nickel.

When I was old enough, my Grandma Richard let me wash dishes for a nickel. I didn't mind the pay back then because it was enough to buy a pop. My mom would probably have liked for me to have had a little of that enthusiasm at home. When we saved up enough money from doing chores, at least a nickel or a dime, we would walk down to Shimer's store.

This crossroads store was also Munday's post office and gas station, all in one. At the crossroads, you could either go left to Calhoun County toward Grantsville, or you could go right to Bell School and on over to Elizabeth, or you could go back the way we came which would take you all the way to Parkersburg.

I enjoyed these walks to the store and back, especially seeing the flowers that bloomed along the creek bank or on the hillsides. Walking to the store, the creek bank was on our left and the hillside was on our right. The tiger lily was aptly named as it was dark orange with black dots or specks, and grew abundantly along the ditches and creek banks. Trilliums had a white or pink lily-like blossom with three large green leaves, and it grew in thick patches along the hillside. We would pass the houses of our neighbors, who often waved to us if they were out in their yards or sitting on their front porches. Several of the people who lived along the Munday road were not only neighbors, but good friends or relatives. We didn't have to worry about walking along the road by ourselves when we were children. There wasn't a need for neighborhood watches or police patrols.

Grandma Richard sent her grocery list with us one day and we gave it to Mr. Shimer, who filled her order, much like you would see Ike Godsey on *The Waltons.* We carried the groceries back to Grandma in a brown paper bag. When she opened the bag and started going through her groceries, she burst out laughing. There amongst her regular order was a tin can of Half & Half tobacco. She had ordered half and half cream but didn't specify that on the list, and we were too busy with our purchases - candy and pop – to notice. We all got the biggest laugh out of that transaction because if you had known my Grandma Richard, you would realize how terribly bizarre that purchase would have been for her. Needless to say, Mr. Shimer traded the Half & Half for Grandma and all was well.

Saturday Morning Cartoons

Saturday morning cartoons have changed dramatically since I was a child. A look at the 1990s gives you a broad spectrum of how cartoons have changed from one year to the next – from *Winnie the Pooh* and *Alvin and the Chipmunks* in the early '90s, to cartoons and TV shows with monsters and warriors in the late '90s. The latter depicts the more violent and aggressive turn television has taken. I'm thankful for the kind of Saturday morning cartoons we grew up with in the 1960s.

It was so exciting to get our first television set as a child. We only had three channels to choose from, no cable back then, but we didn't think of that as limited. Dad put an antenna up on the hill for good reception. Sometimes when we had bad weather, it would blow the antenna around and our television screen would be all "snowy" – we couldn't see a thing.

We couldn't stay up late during the week to watch it as we had school the next day, but we enjoyed Saturday morning cartoons. How could anyone who was a child during that era forget *Touche Turtle and Dum Dum*, that heroic fencing pair who battled villains and saved kings, queens and maidens in distress?

Wally Gator was a friendly alligator who looked as harmless as a fly and who felt more comfortable when he was at home, in the city zoo. The zookeeper kept a close eye on Wally, however, as he sometimes escaped to check out things away from the zoo.

I also like *The Jetsons* and *The Flintstones.* My brother, Joe's, favorite was *Foghorn Leghorn.* He was a very large rooster with a loud, overbearing voice like his namesake. He had a hankering for mischief, and most of his pranks involved a barnyard dog, with Foghorn usually coming out on the losing end. I can still hear Joe mocking Foghorn in that deep voice, "I say…I say…that's a joke, son" and then he'd burst out laughing.

Making Cookies with Grandma

Grandma Richard had a special-handled, light green glass mixing bowl that she and I often used to make brown sugar cookies. She was very precise in the method of mixing cookie dough. It was important to cream the butter and brown sugar until light and fluffy before adding any other ingredients, like eggs and flour. I think I can still smell that lovely scent of brown sugar cookies baking in her kitchen.

Grandma's daughters, Lyla and Louise, long remembered her brown sugar cookies, and we often reminisced about how good they were. Her recipe is still around, but try as we might we just can't make them like she could. However, it is one of many fond memories of spending precious moments with my grandma.

Staying Overnight with Grandma

Grandma Richard let me stay overnight with her quite often. Sometimes I slept with her in her bed, but sometimes I slept in the small bedroom next to hers. She woke me around 9 in the morning with these familiar words, "It's time to get up — it's nearly noon."

I suppose 9a.m. would seem late to a woman like Grandma who was used to raising a farming family, and making homemade biscuits and a full breakfast before the sun rose. She cooked three meals a day; work hands got hungry. Grandma was used to having her own milk cows. I remember her telling me how she used to churn butter in the big, gray churn by the door.

I must have been having a bad dream one night, because I kicked the window out by the bed during the night and didn't even know it until the next morning. I was sleeping in the spare room next to Grandma's and she didn't hear me. She didn't get excited over things like that. Dad fixed the window and everything was fine.

During the afternoons, Grandma and I would sit together on her couch in the living room, although she referred to it as the davenport, an old-timey term for it, and watch her favorite soap opera. I still remember those familiar words at the beginning of the show, "Like the sands in an hourglass, so are *The Days of Our Lives.*" She would get the big box of Mister Bee potato chips down from on top of the refrigerator, and untie the plastic bag inside, and we munched on chips while finding out who married who, or who ran out on who on that day's episode… I thought those Mr. Bee potato chips were the best in the world, and they are only made in Parkersburg, West Virginia, my birthplace.

I liked to go in the back bedroom when Uncle Denzil wasn't home. It was his room, but I don't think he minded because I didn't really bother anything. I liked to get the songbook down from on top of his dresser and sing all by myself. I remember *Home on the Range* and *Tom Dooley:*

"..Home, home on the range
Where the deer and the antelope play
Where seldom is heard a discouraging word
And the skies are not cloudy all day…"

and

"…Hang down your head, Tom Dooley
Hang down your head and cry
Hang down your head, Tom Dooley
Poor boy, you're bound to die…"

I sang those songs over and over, and it must have sounded pitiful to Grandma if she had been in the living room where she could hear me. She probably busied herself in the kitchen, out of earshot.

Sometimes at night when we watched television, we often enjoyed a snack of oyster crackers and a glass of cold milk before going to bed.

I watched scary late movies on New Year's Eve with Grandma Richard and Uncle Denzil one year. Grandma and I were sitting on the edge of the couch, really enthralled with a movie, when Uncle Denzil, who was sitting in his favorite chair just a few feet away, yelled "Boo!" Grandma and I nearly came up off the couch. Uncle Denzil thought it was such a good joke. He sat there and laughed and laughed.

Grandma had a big straw hat that she wore when she worked in her garden. She wore long sleeves to protect her arms from the bean vines. Oh, but she loved her green beans, and canned several jars every year. I don't think anybody enjoyed green beans any better than she did. Half Runners, they were called. I remember sitting with her out on the front porch in her glider, stringing green beans (a glider was similar to a swing in a way, it was made of metal and it "glided" back and forth more smoothly than a swing).

Mom and Dad often made us go to bed between 8 and 9 p.m. on weeknights so we could get our rest, and be ready for the next school day. It would often still be daylight when we went to bed, and I remember looking out the window and wondering why it was our bedtime if Grandma was outside working in her garden.

Making Doll Clothes

Grandma Richard gave me scraps of material to make clothes for my dolls. Well, I didn't actually sew. Instead, I cut out a round piece of cloth for a hat and pinned it on the doll's head with a stickpin. Then, I cut out neck and arm holes from a piece of material to match and I would slip the "dress" over the doll's head. My cousin, Teresa, was in with her family from Indiana one summer, and she sat on Grandma's front steps with me and made doll clothes.

I took my dolls' clothes down to the creek and washed them, and gave the dolls a bath. The water wasn't very deep at the time, and it was clear, because we could see the rocks at the bottom, and the fish swimming, so we weren't afraid. I had a laundry day, just like Mom's wash day. I brought the clean clothes back up in the yard and hung everything on Mom's clothesline to dry.

I coaxed my younger brother, Jay, to play dolls with me, since I didn't have any sisters or any little girls nearby to play with. Jay wasn't crazy about the idea, and probably wouldn't have wanted any of his friends to know about it, but I guess he was bored, or maybe he just felt sorry for me.

The Cigar Box

On occasion, Grandma Richard took me with her to Elizabeth, Wirt County's county seat, to visit Aunt Ethel and Uncle Ralph. They were my great-great aunt and uncle. Aunt Ethel was Grandma's aunt on her father's side of the family. Edna's dad, Grandpa Pepper, and Aunt Ethel were brothers and sisters.

Grandma was cold-natured and often wore a short, bolero-style, white sweater over her dresses. She wore a sweater clip with it when she was going somewhere, like to visit Uncle Ralph and Aunt Ethel. The sweater clip held her sweater together, because that style didn't have buttons. There were glistening pink stones on each clip with tiny pearls on the attached chain. It was very pretty, and I always admired it.

Uncle Ralph and Aunt Ethel lived in town. Their house was a big white house with a wrap-around porch. Sometimes we sat on the porch and watched the people as they drove by in their cars or as they walked by on the sidewalk in front of the house.

Grandma saw some young girls walking down the sidewalk in scantily-clad bathing suits one day, and she said they didn't have anything more on than a hair net (of course, a hair net was thin and you could see right through it). She thought it was disgraceful how they paraded up and down in public and it made her want to reach over and jerk their bikini bottoms right off!

Grandma and I would walk down the street to Roberts' store to shop while we were there. To a country girl, Elizabeth seemed like a big town, but it was just a small town with a high school, courthouse, post office, gas station, a few grocery stores, and a small restaurant.

Grandma got her permanents at the beauty shop in Elizabeth. It took hours and hours for the woman to roll her hair in those tiny little curlers with the thin paper liners. I remember waiting for the longest time for Grandma's permanent to be processed. She would get so tired. She had to put her hair up in soft rollers when she got home so her hair would have a softer wave.

One time I went with Grandma, Aunt Ethel had a surprise waiting for me. She had fixed up a whole cigar box of pencils, rubber bands, rain bonnets, and all kinds of things a little girl might like to play with. It was probably things she just had on hand, but I felt so rich and so proud of my little cigar box. It was so thoughtful of her to do that for me. She couldn't have bought me anything that I would have been more proud of. I've thought of that cigar box time and again since my childhood days, and remember my aunt with fondness.

Aunt Ethel, as well as her house, was very neat and clean, and I was surprised to find out that she rubbed snuff and had a brass spittoon sitting beside her chair. When my brother Jay went with us to visit her, she invited him to rub snuff with her.

Wirt County Journal

While reminiscing over some old letters and cards, I found an old copy of the *Wirt County Journal*, the local county paper, folded up in the lining of my memory box. It was crumpled and brown after forty-odd years. It was dated Thursday, May 2, 1968. A verse right under the heading of the paper which read, *"How beautiful upon the mountains are the feet of him that bringeth good tidings..." (Isaiah 52:7)*

It was interesting to see how much grocery prices varied from what they were back then. *Dick's Market* advertised Friday and Saturday specials: All-meat bologna – 39 cents a pound; Sandwich bread – two loaves for 49 cents; two-pound package of French fries – 3/$1.00; twelve ounces Armour's Treat – 49 cents; one pound package of Blue Bonnet Oleo – 4/$1.00; ten-ounce jar Smuckers Raspberry Jelly – 35 cents; Pillsbury cake mixes – 3/$1.00; and five-pound bag of oranges – 59 cents. *Sims & George* grocery store advertised: Banquet dinners – 39 cents each; Picnic hams – 39 cents a pound; Eggs – 39 cents a dozen; Banquet cream pies – three for 89 cents; green onions – 10 cents a bunch and fresh cabbage – 10 cents a pound.

Under the community column, *"Brohard Times,"* I was surprised to read about my Aunt Frona and her daughter: *"Mrs. Frona Munday returned home Sunday after two weeks at the home of Mr. and Mrs. Earl Hayhurst (Eleanore Mills), of Wheeling. Eleanore had been a hospital surgical patient, and is now home and doing fine."* And I also read about a distant relative of ours, Noble Busch (everybody called him Nobe) – *"Those attending a ham supper at the Co-op Building at MacFarlan Friday evening were Mrs. Clara Bennett, Mr. & Mrs. K.W. Fox, Mr. & Mrs. Curt Simmons, and Mr. & Mrs. Noble Busch."*

Under the classified section, I read how much the cost of cars changed. State Auto Sales advertised: "This Week's Specials – '67 Camaro Conv. - $2,495, '64 Pontiac - $1,195, and a '63 Chevy II Wagon - $895."

County Fair

One of the highlights of late summer was the Wirt County Fair. We were excited to go to the fair at Camp Barbe on Route 14, just outside of Elizabeth, and hear the carnival music as we pulled into the fairgrounds. The fair consisted of carnival rides, games, contests and feasting on candy apples and cotton candy. When I was little, I always liked picking up the little yellow ducks out of the water, and looking on the underneath side to see what number I had drawn; or pitching coins, trying to get them to land in the little glass dishes and tossing rings around a soda pop bottle, trying to win a stuffed animal from all the colorful ones hanging up on display at the booths.

For the adults at the fair, there was the Quilt Contest to see who would win the prize ribbons for the most beautiful ones entered; the Art Contest for drawings and paintings, and crafts of all designs and ideas. Rows and rows of jams and jellies, applesauce, green beans, and any number of home canned goods in mason jars lined the display tables for the local judges to decide who would take home the red, white, and blue ribbons.

The men and boys especially enjoyed the livestock show or the Pig Chasing Contest. Live entertainment, with various singers including Bluegrass bands and Gospel groups, filled the air. And of course, the Miss Wirt County Fair Princess Pageant was always a highlight of the fair.

For adults and children alike, there were the bingo games, a nice chance to sit down and rest from the various activities of the day.

The Horseshoe Pitching Contest, the Crosscut Saw Contest, the Arm Wrestling Contest, the Skillet Throwing Contest, the Hay Bale Throwing Contest, and the Nail Driving Contest challenged your strength and endurance, as well as a little skill.

There was a Pretty Baby Contest, and who could forget the 100-Foot Banana Split; what a treat for everyone at the fair. The grand finale of the week, and perhaps the most exciting, was the fireworks display on Saturday, the closing night of the fair. (The Wirt County Fair has been around for fifty years, nearly as long as I have).

Crossing the Fence

My brothers and I loved to walk down to Lula's, a kind neighbor who was like family. Lula lived just down the path from us, but Mom warned us not to go by ourselves, and NOT to cross her fence since there were cattle and a mean bull in her pasture. The pasture was so green, partly flat and partly hilly, and we thought it was beautiful. It drew us, despite our efforts to resist. We were determined to cross that fence, so we slipped away one day and headed down the path. When we got to Lula's and crossed over, we heard Uncle Ross from across the road hollering at us, "Get out of there!" It scared him to see children in the pasture with the bull, but we didn't see the danger.

When Mom discovered we were gone, she came hurrying down the path after us with fire in her eyes. When she got hold of us, we wished we had heeded the warning instead of being so hardheaded. We marched back up the path with sore backsides, learning our lesson the hard way. No more fence crossing for us.

Older Brother Pranks

My older brother, Joe, with his crew cut haircut (which I thought resembled the bristle surface of a brush), white T-shirt, and blue jeans rolled up at the cuffs, was a menace. He wasn't afraid of snakes and he took pleasure in tormenting me. He caught black snakes and put them on a stick or fishing pole where he could hold them up and display them like some trophy he had just won. He chased me with them all over our yard and Grandma's, laughing as he went.

When we lived in our little house at Munday, my bed was in the living room, but the boys had a bedroom with bunk beds. Their bedroom was close enough for us to talk back and forth after we had gone to bed. One night when I was very young, Joe told me a tale about a huge snake that was as wide as the road and as long as the distance from our house to Grantsville, which was about a half-hour away. When I realized that he was just making that all up, he laughed and laughed and laughed. He thought it was such a good joke.

Sunday School Supper at Lula's

Lula Wilson was not only our neighbor, but also my Sunday school teacher at the little white Methodist church in Munday, which was located beside Bell School.

Lula was short of stature with pretty white hair that she wore up in a bun. When she was at home, we were used to seeing her wearing her pretty, homemade aprons. She raised a vegetable garden and beautiful flowers. Her lovely dahlias were my favorites. She often picked bouquets and brought them to us or Grandma Richard. I often walked down to her house and stood by the fence, admiring her dahlias which grew up the side, near the window.

One day, I asked Lula if she had any saltine crackers, and she gave me some to snack on. When Mom found out I had asked for food, she was so upset and scolded me. She didn't want folks thinking I went without at home. I could have been hungry for crackers, but most likely hungrier for her company, as I loved Lula so.

Lula was married to Orlan Wilson, and they had a daughter named Delta Pearl. As Delta Pearl was away in the military, I don't remember much about her. While Orlan was out hunting one day, his rifle discharged while he was crossing a fence, and tragically he died.

Lula was such a caring person, and I'm glad she was our teacher. My Sunday school classmates at the little Methodist church were Helen and Donnie. We didn't have separate rooms for Sunday school classes; we had heavy drapes that were drawn to separate the children's classes from the adult's. The dark, upright piano was on the left side of the church, and there was a heating stove on the right side. The wooden benches, or pews, were lined up through the center, and on either side of the church, allowing for two short aisles. The children's classes were at the front, on either side of the pulpit.

I was very excited to be invited to supper at Lula's house for just us young people; it made me feel special. I was to be polite and on my best behavior. Mom instructed me to be sure to thank Lula for inviting me and for a nice supper, but instructed me to wait until after supper to tell her. I was so worried I might forget, I just blurted it out right there during the meal and had three pairs of eyes looking at me, much to my embarrassment. They probably felt as awkward as I did.

I can't remember exactly what Lula cooked for supper that day, but she was a wonderful cook, and I remember her pies and cakes, too. She made us a special cake for that evening. It was a sheet cake with white icing, trimmed in a light-blue-turquoise color and designs were drawn across the cake. That was a very special evening, and I hold the memory dear in my heart.

Parkersburg, WV

On Saturdays, Dad and Mom occasionally took us shopping in Parkersburg, a town about thirty miles away. Parkersburg was a lot bigger than Elizabeth, and there were more stores to choose from.

We shopped for school clothes there, although Mom made some of ours, and we shopped for Christmas presents near the holiday.

We were so used to our small community that we had no need for a traffic light; everyone just knew to slow down at the crossroads. So, seeing the lights and hearing the sounds of the big city, was quite foreign to us, and very exciting, especially at Christmastime when we saw the brightly decorated shop windows and Christmas lights.

We loved for Dad to take us to the Big Boy restaurant where we could get ten hamburgers for a dollar. They tasted so good. I looked forward to our outings in Parkersburg.

When Joe was about six years old, he had to have an operation to have his tonsils removed. Mom and Dad took him to St. Joseph's Hospital in Parkersburg (that's also where I was born in December 1957). The Catholic Nuns were very strict, and wouldn't let Mom stay in the room with Joe, which upset her very much. They did let her hold him when they brought him out of surgery, and the ether they used to put him to sleep was still so strong, Mom said it nearly knocked *her* out.

'57 Chevy

I remember Dad's 1957 Chevy, a four-door, Bel Air sedan. It was a shiny two-tone, light mauve and white – a real looker. He parked it over by the road as we had a footbridge to walk across, but not a bridge to drive across the creek. Someone must have dropped off the berm one day and hit the car because the back rear driver's side of the car was smashed. My younger brother Jay, when he was about five years old, was photographed standing beside the car after it had been hit.

Mom told me of another 1957 Chevy that Dad had. It was a Bel Air, two-door coupe – robin's egg blue and white; a beautiful car, and quite the rage back then. I can picture Dad taking Mom to the Mt. Zion Drive-in out on Rt. 16 in that sporty car.

Chapter 3

Calhoun County: Folklore, Floods, and Family Ties

Sampson P. Rose & Hazel (Munday) Rose

My Great-grandpa Sampson P. Rose (b. June 3, 1880) married Hazel Munday (b. March 3, 1894). Grandpa Rose's parents were James A. Rose and Sarah Ellen (Boice) Rose. His father, James, was born about 1841 in Virginia and was a Civil War Veteran (1861-1865). His mother, Sarah, was born in 1852 in Virginia.

Grandma Hazel Rose's parents were George Washington Munday (known as "Wash") and Anna (Slater) Munday. Grandma's father, George, was born in 1861, and her mother, Anna, was born in 1868. Grandma Rose's grandparents (Anna's parents), Janet and George Slater, came from Germany. They came by boat to America; the boat had huge sails, and it was a seven-week voyage. They first settled in Pittsburgh, Pennsylvania; then came by boat and settled on Rt. 16 in Calhoun County, West Virginia, along the Little Kanawha River (across the river from where my Great-grandparents, Sampson and Hazel Rose, were to build their home).

Hazel had a sister named Effie (Munday) Mills, and five brothers, Kenneth Virgil (we called him Uncle "Virge" – he was married to Aunt Faye, who was the cook at Bell School), Ross, Frank, Glenn, and Leonard.

Grandpa and Grandma Rose lived on the banks of the Little Kanawha River just above the bend at Industry, West Virginia. Grandpa Rose, "Samp," (as he was known) was a mail carrier who had a route from Industry to

MacFarlan, about twenty miles away. He drove a hackney, better known as a horse and buggy, and was similar to what the Amish used. Even in the wintertime when the snow fell really hard, he just bundled up and took off on his route as the mail had to go through.

Grandpa Rose had another job, running a boat which transported groceries on the Little Kanawha River from Industry all the way to the store in Annamoriah, about ten or fifteen miles away. He occasionally took his daughter, Nona (my Grandma Maze), with him on his route. They cooked meals on the boat, and he let Nona help wash the dishes, which made a little girl feel really important and useful.

Hazel was well known for her quilting. She crafted beautiful quilts and sold them to help with the family income. She had a crippled hand that was drawn up since she was a child, but still quilted by hand, raised a garden, and did the canning.

Hazel also took in boarders. She cooked their meals and packed their lunches. She cooked on a big wood stove with a water heater (reservoir) on the side. The water was heated there to wash dishes. The water was drawn up in buckets from the well; they also caught rainwater to use.

I never knew my Great-grandpa Sampson Rose as he passed away February 11, 1957, and I was born in December of that year. I vaguely remember my Great-grandma Hazel Rose, but Mom remembers her well. I have a picture of Great-grandpa Rose sitting in a chair at their house at Christmas, opening presents. He had on suspenders as men often wore in those days, and he was wearing a cap. Great-grandma Rose was a stout woman who wore her hair pulled back, as was the custom. She had a very pleasant face. Another good photo I have of them was from 1943; Grandpa had on a suit and tie and Grandma was wearing a coat over her dress and was wearing heels. They were standing on a dirt road with a rocky hill as a backdrop.

Hazel had a vegetable garden, and I remember their big wrap-around porch. You could walk just a few steps from their porch down to the riverbank. Mom recalls that Grandma Rose's flowers were something to behold. She had a big garden of flowers growing at the end of the house, nearest the road, and it stretched down the path along the edge of the yard, a beautiful welcome to anyone coming to visit. Among her flowers were the coleus, cockscomb, petunias, live forever, scarlet sage, and of course, roses. Some of the flowers grew so big that they were taller than Grandma's head. She had purple clematis climbing up the post on the wraparound porch, and flowers of various kinds in pots adorning the porch banisters.

Mom as a Girl Growing Up in Calhoun County

Mom was born in 1936 and grew up near the little community of Big Bend in Calhoun County, West Virginia, not far from Industry. Her father worked for Cabot Gas and was away from home much of the time. Her mother stayed at home, raising her, her two sisters and three brothers. They worked hard planting a large garden, and canning food for the winter months ahead.

Mom liked to go muskrat trapping with her Grandpa Rose. He kept a johnboat down at the river, near his house. Mom was probably about nine or ten years old when her grandpa would let her sit in the back seat of the boat and paddle for him while he checked his muskrat traps near the riverbank. He took the muskrats home and stretched them out on a special board for them to dry. Later, he sold the pelts to fur buyers, which helped supplement the family income.

Mom and her brothers and sisters walked the dirt road for two or three miles to school. Walking that far to school today would probably seem outrageous to most children, but back then they didn't think anything of it because they had to walk to get most places. If there was a family vehicle, it was usually used by the father to go off to work. When the children got down to Leading Creek, near their Grandpa and Grandma Rose's, they had to climb a rocky road up a very steep hill to the white one-room schoolhouse. Mom's first teacher was Will Collins. Mr. Collins lived near the general store at Industry, not far from the school. He was an older man with gray hair, glasses, and a stern manner. He was so strict that he didn't pass Mom in the first grade. She had to take it over. The next year, they got a new teacher, Agnes Cain, who was very nice, and made learning enjoyable for the children. Mom had no trouble advancing at the end of that year.

Grandpa Rose had a potato patch near the school. He harvested the potatoes with a horse and plow, and the children liked to help pick up the potatoes during recess. He loaded the potatoes up on a big wooden sled and hauled them off the steep hill to be placed in his cellar to keep through the winter.

There was a big house near the school where Asa and Flora Maze lived. Their yard adjoined the schoolyard. At Easter time, Flora hid eggs for the school children. She hid them around the house and in the flower beds, and one place in particular that Mom remembered her hiding them was in the pockets of the coats she hung on her clothesline. The children had such a good time hunting the Easter eggs.

For the children's drinking water, there was a dug well out in the school yard with a bucket tied to a rope they lowered down into the well to draw up the water. The children liked to pull up the bucket from the well and pour it into another bucket; then it was carried inside and poured it into the big stone jar to keep cool. The jar had a spigot on the side which allowed them to run the water into their little tin cups.

Mom went to that school for about two years, but eventually they closed it down, and the children transferred to Brooksville School at Big Bend, which was between their house and Grantsville, the county seat. The bus came part of the way to pick them up, but they had to walk down a hill to catch it. Their schoolhouse at Brooksville was up on a hill, but it wasn't quite as steep a climb as it was to the other school. This school was a two-room school and went through the eighth grade.

Blaine didn't like his teacher, Mrs. Hathaway, when he was in the second or third grade. He had to get on the bus with the other children in the morning, but he would slip off once he got to Brooksville and walk back home. If their dad was home, he would take him back to school. Mom remembered two of her teachers, John Yoke and Mrs. Cain who transferred from Mom's first school. Icie Jones and Mildred Smith were the cooks. Mom didn't like anything made with beef, so if they were having something like vegetable beef soup for lunch, they were kind enough to cook something else for her, like boiled potatoes. In the mornings, the bus driver would let the children off at Holbert's store, at the bottom of the hill, just below the schoolhouse. Mom recalled taking an egg to Holbert's and trading it for a paper bag full of candy. The storekeepers could always use eggs and didn't mind trading with the children. Sometimes, the children saved their egg money, and in the afternoons after school, they would stop in at Holbert's for an ice cream cone. They liked Harvey Cottrell to wait on them because he gave the children double scoops.

At Easter, Mom and her brothers and sisters made their own Easter baskets out of the big oat boxes. They cut the box about halfway down, saving enough to make a bail. To decorate, they cut up crepe paper into tiny pieces, like confetti. They cooked flour, sugar, and water to make their own paste; once the paste was cool, they pasted the tiny pieces of crepe paper on their baskets. They filled the baskets with Easter grass, and placed colored eggs on the grass. Their mom helped them color the eggs with food coloring that she had in her cupboard. The children placed their Easter baskets on the front steps on the night before Easter Sunday. Mom remembered her parents going down to Grandpa and Grandma Rose's the night before Easter, and the Easter Bunny always came while they were gone. They found big candy eggs in a rainbow of colors in their baskets. The candy eggs had a hard shell on the outside with a soft white marshmallow on the inside. Her mom and dad managed to slip the candy into their baskets on the way down the steps, but the children never saw them.

Mom and Dad continued an Easter tradition with my brothers and me. Every year on Easter morning, we woke up to find three Easter baskets on the kitchen table; each one had Easter grass, Easter eggs that Mom had helped us color with food coloring, a chocolate Easter bunny, and some tiny chocolate candies shaped like eggs, or footballs as we liked to call them, and a bottle of our favorite soda pop sitting beside each basket. Even into our teen years, it was a treat for Mom and Dad to remember this tradition by giving us a basket like we had when we were children, and always with a bottle of pop.

At Halloween, Mom and her brothers and sisters made their own masks and costumes; they didn't go to the store and buy that type of things back then. They starched white muslin until it was real stiff; then pulled it down over a mold. Sometimes they would turn a bowl upside down and pull the muslin down over it to mold it into a mask that could later be colored or decorated. For costumes, they dressed up in their parents' clothes or clothes that were too big for them; sometimes they used sheets to make their costumes. They decorated brown paper bags to make their own treat bags. They went Trick-or-Treating to the houses in the neighborhood, usually starting at their Grandma Sarah Maze's across the road, and then heading out the ridge to their Aunt Lucille's and up on the hill to Grace Maze's before venturing down the Munday road to Grandma and Grandpa Rose's. Their treat bags would be loaded down with apples, candy, and popcorn balls when they arrived back home. Their mom let them help make molasses taffy in the fall, and sometimes they had it around Halloween. To make old-fashioned molasses taffy, they cooked molasses, butter, sugar, water, and corn syrup in a big kettle over high heat until the sugar dissolved; then poured it out on a big buttered pan; as the edges cooled, they turned it with a spatula; then they buttered their hands and two of them at a time would pull the candy, stretching it into a long rope; once it had turned light in color, they cut it into pieces and wrapped it in wax paper (what wasn't eaten at the time, of course).

At Christmas, although their family didn't have a lot of money, their dad, Clarence Maze Sr., always tried to see that the children had something from Santa. When Mom and her brothers and sisters were young, their mother always sent them across the road to their Grandma Sarah Maze's on Christmas Eve (Grandpa Joseph Maze had passed away when Mom was less than a year old). Her grandma lived in a two-story weatherboarding house; the inside was wallpapered and heated with woodstoves. One year, Mom remembered being over at her grandma's house; she was not supposed to be looking out the window, but curiosity got the better of her. She saw Santa (her dad) with a big white toboggan on his head, going over the hill to the garage; he took their presents out of the garage and loaded them into a big white sack he carried over his shoulder; he continued up the hill to their house, where he delivered the packages under their Christmas tree.

Their mother came out on the porch and yelled across the road to the children, "Santa Claus came! Santa Claus came!"

The children tore out of their grandma's house and ran across the road in the snow to see what treasures Santa brought them. There were new clothes, and the girls had books of cutout paper dolls; the boys had marbles and Jacks, and they all had treats to eat – peanuts, oranges and tangerines, and the haystacks and bonbon candies were their favorite.

One year, when Mom was about twelve, after she stopped believing in Santa Claus, her dad bought coloring books for her and her sister, Betty. The two girls fought over the coloring books, and they both got a whipping from their dad, which was rare. He worked for Cabot Gas and was away from home most of the time, so he didn't get to see the children very often.

Aunt Minnie Maze and Uncle Brady Davis (pronounced BRAD-EEE which is short for Bradford), were brother and sister on Grandpa Maze's side of the family. They lived behind them out the ridge, about a mile or so from where Mom and her family lived. Aunt Minnie lived in an old weatherboarding house with a kitchen, living room, and three, small bedrooms. There was a dug well on the back porch (they dug a well and then built the porch around it), and an outhouse across the yard. Uncle Brady lived in the building above the cellar, which he had converted into living quarters with a small bed, a cook stove, and a table. Aunt Minnie was a short, heavyset woman with dark hair who wore bibbed aprons over her dresses. She had to burn coal to cook and heat the house. The coal dust settled into her skin for so long that her arms appeared dirty. Uncle Brady was also heavyset and taller than his sister. He usually wore bibbed overalls, an overall jacket, and a straw hat.

There was an apple orchard a few yards from Aunt Minnie's, and she had fallen in the orchard one day and couldn't get up. Mom had gone out the ridge to check on her, and found her there. She ran all the way back home to get help. When they got Aunt Minnie back in the house, she was so thankful Mom had found her and went for help that she wanted to give her something in return. She didn't have much to offer her, but to show her gratitude, she gave her a big wooden spoon and a kitchen grater she had hanging on her wall.

Uncle Brady used to fix pancakes for Mom and her brothers and sisters when they went to visit. But, when he got older and his mind started failing him, he didn't act as rationally as he once had. Sometimes, the children would be visiting Aunt Minnie, and he would come in the house and chase them around the table, which scared the daylights out of them. They always managed to escape somehow, and ran all the way back home, glancing over their shoulders as they went. I can almost hear their bare feet hitting the dirt road. Sometimes at night, Uncle Brady would walk out the ridge and sit on Mom's front porch. She recalls Grandma Maze getting up early in the morning and looking out to see Uncle Brady sitting in the rocking chair. It scared Grandma Maze half to death.

Uncle Brady always wore a hat, and one day while he was at Mom's house, he misplaced it and refused to go home without it. They were at wits end to know what to do. Finally, Mom's brother, Junior found an old hat and asked Uncle Brady, "Is this your hat, Uncle Brady?" He replied, "I'd hate to think so."

Aunt Minnie had a daughter, Goldie May, who died as an infant, and a son, Freddie, who died as a teenager. She also had a son, Okey, who Mom remembered. He married Reva Pettit, Sherman Pettit's sister.

Aunt Minnie's daughter, Blanche ("Dixie" as they knew her), married, and she and her husband traveled and sang. Their duo was called "Speed and Dixie." Mom and her brothers saw Okey and his wife occasionally, but rarely saw Dixie as she and her husband were on the road, traveling and singing.

Mom's brother Clarence, Jr., known as Junior to the family, was forever playing tricks when they were young. One day in the mid-1940s, he decided to play a trick on Grace Maze who lived up on the hill, across the road from them. He dressed up in overalls with an overall jacket and straw hat like Uncle Brady wore. He walked across the road where his grandparents used to live, but they had passed on by then. Grace looked down over the hill, and saw a man dressed in overalls and wearing a straw hat, but she wasn't close enough to see his face; he carried what looked like an ax in his hand and stood outside the old barn.

"Glen, you better go see if you can help that pour old soul get back home," she yelled to her husband.

She thought it was Uncle Brady, and that he probably had wandered off again. Glen went over the hill, but soon found out that it was just Junior dressed up and playing a joke. Glen and "Uncle Brady," carrying the ax, went into the barn and didn't emerge for a long time. They sat visiting, while Grace's mind raced, wondering what happened to her husband. The Maze family got a big laugh out of it, and the story was told again and again.

One thing Mom and her family always had plenty of was food, as they worked hard and took it from the land. They raised a big vegetable garden, a large cornfield, and potato patch. When their dad was home one summer, and the children had finished hoeing the corn field, Mom remembers him going to the general store and buying them each a pint of ice cream, which was a real treat for them. Store-bought food always was.

One of their neighbors wanted to bake a special cake for company they were expecting, but her oven wasn't working so she asked Grandma Maze if she could use hers. Mom came in from playing outside and saw the cake on the table. It smelled so good she couldn't resist. She reached up with her little hand and grabbed a fistful. She must have been about four or five at the time. Her mom became very upset when she saw what she had done. The neighbor just got tickled at the little girl and wouldn't allow her to be spanked or punished in any way.

This is just an example of the community raising their children and the good sense of humor they had. They truly loved their neighbors, and wanted the children to turn out well.

When Mom was about nine or ten, her mother had to go in the hospital and have an operation. She had to place her children in separate homes in the community, dividing them among friends and relatives during the week she was away. Blaine was the youngest of six children. Mom always took up for him and babied him. She was sent to stay with her Aunt Lucille, across the road and out the ridge from them. However, Mom snuck out and went up on the hill to Grace Maze's to see Blaine. She was not used to being separated from her brother.

They lived on one side of the hill and Grace and her family lived on the other. Mom remembered Grace making big bowls of mashed potatoes, creamed tomatoes, and skillets of corn bread for them.

Grandpa Rose had a cane patch across the road, and nearly in sight of their house, and Mom remembered sorghum molasses making time. While watching the day's process, the children had a board across a rock that they were using as a make-do teeter-totter. Mom sat on one end when Grandpa Rose sat down on the other side, flipping Mom, who was just a little girl at the time, up in the air. She jumped off that teeter-totter and said to him, "Don't do that again, Mister!"

This about tickled her Grandpa Rose nearly half to death.

The cane plants were ready for harvesting in late September or early October. Very few people had their own mills years ago, usually only one in a neighborhood. The size of the cane patches would depend on how much a family needed. If they planted just enough for their family, a small patch would produce anywhere from ten to twelve gallons. Sugar wasn't plentiful back then, so a good crop of cane was important. To extract the juice from the cane, a horse was harnessed to a pole, and the horse walked around in circles. The pole was attached to gears which turned the rollers of the mill. The horse was usually trained to start and stop as they called out to it. It had to keep a slow, steady pace while walking around and around. If the horse they used wasn't properly trained, someone would have to lead it around to keep it from tearing up their mill or possibly hurting someone. The juice from the cane was squeezed out and ran down into a pan; then they cooked it into the dark, sweet molasses. The molasses were poured into gallon stone jugs which kept them well through the winter months. If the liquid happened to turn back to sugar by spring, all they had to do was get the jug out of the cellar and put it on the back of the stove to heat up, and then it would pour just as well as it did when it was first made.

Besides pouring the molasses on biscuits, it was used in baking cookies and cakes, to sweeten pumpkin pies, or to make the popcorn balls Mom remembered Grandma Maze making with them. Mom especially remembered getting to eat the skimmings off the top of the molasses when they were making them. The skimmings was the sweet, foamy top of the molasses. They didn't have a lot of candy and sweets, so this was a real treat.

Wash day at the Maze's was the talk of the community. There were eight in the family, and they only had wash day once a week, so it was a huge undertaking. Grandma had clotheslines strung across the yard, from one end to the other; Mom said she didn't know how many times they filled those lines each wash day. They had an old Maytag washing machine with a gas motor that they had to kick-start. The clothes were run through a ringer to get the excess water out, and all the Maze girls got their hair caught in the ringer at some time or another. Once the clothes were dry, they took them off the line and carried everything inside to be ironed the next day. The old-fashioned irons had to be heated on the stove. The family used several irons so one would be keeping hot on the stove when it was time to switch off. The clothes were spread out on a table for ironing, but eventually they got an ironing board.

During summer break, and when Mom was about eleven or twelve, she worked for Mrs. Harris, a retired health nurse who lived down a dirt road, about a mile from their house. Mr. Harris was a retired school teacher. Mrs. Harris paid Mom a nickel to wash dishes. She must have saved her dishes for a whole week because her sink would be piled high when she got there. Mrs. Harris had a strange way of doing dishes. She not only washed dishes in soapy water, but rinsed them in soapy water, too. That was kind of hard for Mom. She earned a quarter for washing down Mrs. Harris' walls. She did various other chores for her. Mom was saving her money to buy a white blouse she had seen in a store window in Grantsville with a $3 price tag, and was determined to own a store-bought blouse. Mom wanted to own something different than feed-sack clothing. She wore the store-bought blouse, and was proud that she had earned the money herself to buy it.

Mom's Great-Aunt Annie Amos and Great-Uncle Bob Maze, on her dad's side of the family, lived across the road and out the ridge about a mile and a half or so from them, not too far from the Maze family cemetery. Aunt Annie was a widow, and she and her brother, Bob, lived in a two story, gray weatherboarding house. They had several chickens, and Aunt Annie sold the eggs to Shimer's store at Munday. Mom recalled seeing Aunt Annie carrying her big wicker basket full of eggs out to their house and dropping it off until someone from Shimer's store could come by and pick them up. In the summertime, when my dad was a teenager, he helped the Shimer boys make deliveries in their dad's truck. Mom looked forward to seeing the Shimer delivery truck come by, hoping to catch a glimpse of that cute Arlis Richard. When Mom was in her early teens, she worked for Uncle Bob and Aunt Annie. She helped them on Saturdays in the spring when planting time came, and then about once a week in the summertime, doing whatever needed done around the house. She did the laundry in their washing machine with the ringer on the side. They had to carry water from the well out in the yard, and her Uncle Bob helped her bring the water in. She hung the clothes on the clothesline to dry, and the sunshine always gave the laundry a nice, clean smell. She swept and mopped or helped with the canning, whatever needed done that particular week. She remembered helping with the pickled beans. They had to string the green beans, place them in a big, stone jar and pour the salt brine over the beans to sour or pickle the vegetables. To make the salt brine, they put coarse salt in water, add a raw egg in the shell, and if the egg floated, they knew the brine had enough salt. They set the jar in the cellar and left it for about three weeks; then they transferred the beans to half-gallon jars, heated the salt water to stop the pickling process and poured it over the beans, sealed the jars, and kept them in the cellar. Mom remembered helping Aunt Annie plant the beans and corn. The ground was soft and the little furrows plowed in straight rows as Aunt Annie dropped the seeds into the ground with this little rhyme:

"One for the bug,
One for the fly,
One for the Devil,
And one for I"

Uncle Bob paid Mom $5 per week, and for a day or so of work, that was a lot of money back then. Mom said she felt like she was rich.

Al and Winnie Jeffries lived further out the ridge from Aunt Annie and Uncle Bob. Winnie Jeffries was Glen Maze's aunt, and Etta Dewees's sister. (Glen and Grace Maze lived up on the hill opposite Mom's house). Sometimes Mom and her brother, Roger, along with Mary and Billy Maze

(Glen & Grace Maze's children), would walk out the ridge to visit Al and Winnie. To get to their house, they had to pass Aunt Annie and Uncle Bob's and the Maze Cemetery, and then go down over the hill to the river. When they reached the river, they would holler for Al to come and get them in his johnboat. He paddled them across the river and they all walked up the hill to their house. Winnie was a medium build, and always wearing her hair under a dust cap. Al was tall and rather heavyset, wearing bibbed overalls. Sometimes, if they needed groceries, Mom and Roger, along with Mary and Billy, would make the long journey to Annamoriah to the store. The journey was about five miles, over hills and meadows. When Al and Winnie were younger, they raised a garden, but as they got older, they had to depend on their neighbors to bring food in for them.

Back then, neighbors helped neighbors. It was just the thing to do.

The first school known to be held in a cave was in 1818 near Big Bend on the Little Kanawha. Robert Clifford was the first teacher with about a dozen students present. Mom and her family lived near Big Bend, and she would tell me the stories of being in that cave herself when she was about ten or twelve years old. The cave was across the river from their family cemetery – the Maze Cemetery – and around the hill from where Al and Winnie lived. Mom and her brothers and sisters had heard the story, which was handed down to them through the generations.

Indians were said to have lived in that area, near Annamoriah, during the time the first school was held in the cave. Mom saw signs where they'd had fires in the cave. The top of the cave was all smoked up, and there were large rocks in the cave, which they presumed were used for seating.

Mom and her family went to the little white church, Pleasant Valley United Brethren, about a mile from home. Grandma and the girls made their own dresses, and walked to church most of the time unless her dad happened to be home with the family car. They made the dresses out of yard goods bought from the store in Grantsville, when they could afford to. Often times, they would make their dresses from the flowered feed sacks. The scratch for the chickens and the feed for the cows came in pretty, cloth sacks with flowered designs, and it would have been a shame to have thrown the sacks away. Mom played the piano at church when she was about fourteen or fifteen years old. Her oldest brother, Clarence Jr., taught her how to play a few keys on her right hand and the rest she played by ear. Their congregation was probably about forty or so. They were not able to pay the preacher a large salary, but about once a year they had a "pounding" for him. They brought him such things as cured hams, vegetables, and homemade jellies and jams. Somebody once brought a live chicken in a box and set it on the altar. They brought what they had. Several of the church families often took turns inviting the preacher and his wife home with them for Sunday dinner. In the afternoon, they sat on the porch and relaxed and visited.

Mom's brothers made their own sleds. Runners were made out of boards they trimmed at a certain angle; then they nailed boards across the runners; they cut two smaller boards, each about six inches long, and nailed them to the runners for handles to steer the sled. They hooked a rope on the sled to pull it back up the hill. There was a barn below their house where their milk cow, Cherry, was kept. Once, when Mom was sleigh riding down the hill, she got too close to the barbwire fence and went under it and skinned her knees all up.

When a big snow came and there were high drifts, the main roads were closed. Mom and her brothers and sisters could sleigh ride down the hills on the country roads without any worry of passing traffic.

A little further down the hollow from their barn was a duck pond where Mom liked to wander off and watch the ducks swimming in warmer weather. They laid their eggs along the bank around the pond, and Mom would find them among the cattails, the tall reedy marsh plants with the brown furry spikes.

Clarence Jr. went on to college. One of the colleges he attended was Glenville State College in Glenville, West Virginia. He eventually became dean there. Later, he and his wife, Marlene, moved to Virginia, where he became president of Richard Bland College of The College of William and Mary. A dinner was held in The Chesapeake Room at The College of William and Mary on April 11, 1996, where Dr. Clarence Maze, Jr., among others, was honored. This is an excerpt from what they had to say about him and his wife: "Dr. Clarence Maze, Jr. became the second president of Richard Bland College of The College of William and Mary in Virginia on August 1, 1975, and has skillfully led the institution through twenty years of academic, physical, and social progress. As architect of the most recent restructuring plan, he has streamlined the administration and downsized the faculty bureaucracy from five academic divisions to two.

"He has enhanced the curriculum with several innovative programs, including theatre and speech which results in four to five major productions per year. President Maze has also developed the International Studies Program, which makes it possible for students to earn academic credit for international educational travel. He has personally organized and led educational travel trips around the world… Under his leadership, a well-planned and beautifully executed landscape program has been developed which through minimum maintenance provides the entire community with spectacular scenery… President Maze's contributions to the community have been extensive. Dr. Maze will retire on July 31, 1996… Marlene Dotson Maze has served for the past twenty years as the first lady of Richard Bland College. During her tenure, she has consistently demonstrated her enthusiasm and support and has served actively as part of the presidential team. Mrs. Maze brought a thoughtful standard of excellence in her role as College ambassador in visits with alumni, donors, and friends…"

This entire article was also published in their local newspaper with an added paragraph acknowledging their parents.

"Pres. Maze's mother, Mrs. Clarence Maze Sr., resides in Calhoun County, while Mrs. Maze's parents, Mr. and Mrs. Dotson, live in Pennsboro [West Virginia]."

Mom and her other brothers and sisters grew up, married, and some of them moved away from the area. Her sister Betty married and moved to Ohio; as did her sister Connie. Their brother Roger married and moved to Tennessee. My mother, Karen, married and lived in Munday, only about five miles from her childhood home; and Blaine, the youngest, married and moved near Grantsville, about fifteen miles away. Aunt Betty and Uncle Norm lived in Ohio about five years and then moved back to West Virginia. They bought the farm on top of the hill where Asa and Flora Maze had lived years before. The farm, with several acres of land, included the little schoolhouse where Betty and her brothers and sisters had attended as children.

Grandma had taken night classes and received her GED before Grandpa passed away. She became a teacher's aide, starting out at Grantsville, Calhoun's county seat; she went on to Cabot Station and then to Brooksville school at Big Bend, nearer her home (this was a newer school at Brooksville than the one Mom and her brothers and sisters attended). I remember hearing Grandma talking about how she liked to help the children. She had a soft voice, and gentle manner. She was uncomfortable when they put her on the spot a few times teaching in front of the class. They even had her helping out with the cooking when the cook didn't show up. She retired after working with the school system for about fifteen years.

After Grandpa Maze passed away, Blaine was good to look after Grandma. She grew to depend on him, and looked forward to his stopping by to fix something around the house, or just visit for a while. When it came to Grandma's cooking, he wasn't hard to please, but he especially liked Grandma's spaghetti and homemade hot rolls, fresh from the oven. Since Betty lived nearby, she also visited Grandma and called to check on her quite often.

Drive-in Theaters

By the mid-1950s, West Virginia was known as having more than 70 drive-in movie theaters open within the state. Sadly, most theaters closed over the years. However, ten are operating within the Mountain State, providing a romantic and nostalgic alternative under the stars.

The Mount Zion Drive-in on Route 16 in Calhoun County was opened in the 1940s and is noted as being the oldest remaining drive-in operating in the state. Dad took Mom to the Mount Zion Drive-in, out on Mount Zion ridge above Grantsville, back in the early 1950s when they dated. They watched movies on the huge, outside screen with the pole speakers; they still have the nostalgic speakers as well as the newer installed radio sound. Not only was it a romantic place to take a date, but it was also a great value for your dollar, as well as being a non-alcoholic establishment.

In 2009, they advertised admission as only $6 per adult. In the 1960s, Mom and Dad took us to the drive-in as a family, and I remember getting hotdogs from the snack bar. Today, the snack bar is a popular drive-up restaurant with a larger menu and less expensive prices than most traditional movie theaters. The inside, smoke-free restaurant features two pool tables and an affordable menu with items such as their sauce bun for 85 cents; a frozen custard vanilla cone for $1.30; French fries or onion rings for a dollar; candy or cookies for less than a dollar, and many other items including sandwiches, sides, pizza, and of course, popcorn. They advertise their movies starting at dusk, anywhere from 8:30 – 9:15 p.m., depending on the night and the weather conditions, but suggest getting there by 8:30 to catch the entire movie.

The drive-in is an experience unlike any other. If a family wanted to go to the movies, the father or mother didn't have to dress up after a hard day's work, and they could bring the children in their pajamas. The atmosphere of an open-air theater and the food is all part of the fun. As they say, "Life is Better Outside."

Flood of the Mid-1950s

Although flash floods ravaged other parts of the state, Mom recalled the flood of the Little Kanawha River at Leading Creek in the mid-1950s, before I was born, as being the worst she can remember.

Leading Creek was just below Grandma and Grandpa Rose's house. It had rained so much that the river overflowed its banks and covered the main road, just before it gushed its way into the downstairs of their home. They had already moved what they could upstairs when they saw the imposing danger; then, they headed up hill to their daughter Nona's (Grandma Maze's) for safety.

Mom's Uncle Ross, Grandma Rose's son, paddled the johnboat about a half-mile to Industry to meet Mom and Dad. They were coming over from Munday, but that was as far as they could make it before the road was completely covered with water. Uncle Ross brought them to Grandma and Grandpa Rose's to help with the cleanup as soon as the water started receding from the downstairs.

Mom and Dad, as well as neighbors and other family members, helped with the cleanup. It was a tremendous undertaking. Dad had a pump he used to wash down the walls and suck the mud and muck out of the house. The wallpaper downstairs was completely ruined. The cabinets in the kitchen had to be cleared out; everything was destroyed.

The water had gotten in their cellar as well. Mom remembered the health nurse advising them of how much bleach to mix with water for cleaning. They mixed bleach and water in a big galvanized tub out in the yard; then carried the dozens and dozens of jars of canned goods from the cellar to be washed off to kill the germs. The yard was also a muddy mess. Although it was not an ideal place to work, it was all they had available. The floor, as well as the shelves in the cellar, had to be scrubbed before they could restock the jars.

It must have seemed like an impossible task at the time to get the house back to some semblance of normalcy. But when I was born a few years later, no traces of that time was evident. I only remember Grandma Rose with her garden, her flowers in all their glory, the family picnics down by the riverbank, and enjoyable days of sitting on her wraparound porch.

All that remains of the catastrophe of the flood for my mom was the memories of the rising waters, of the pulling together of family and friends, a lot of hard work that was done without thought of repayment, the sense of struggling for survival for her grandmother, and the satisfaction of being there and helping family in time of need.

Chapter 4
Remedies, Rituals, and Reunions

Plowing Potatoes

When we were growing up, my family raised a large garden, which supplied us with fresh vegetables in the summer and home-canned vegetables through the winter. Mom put up corn, green beans, tomato juice, pickles, beets, sauerkraut, and pickled beans as well as pickled corn. The jars were neatly stored on shelves in the cellar located out the path, just behind Grandma Richard's house.

We also raised a whole field of potatoes, our staple crop. The potato field was located between our house and Lula's. Dad borrowed Uncle Virge Munday's horse and plow to harvest the potatoes. I can still smell the pungent earth as Mom, my brothers and I, would go behind Dad and pick up sack after sack of plowed-out potatoes. We had twenty bushels or more when we were done. Dad hauled them to the cellar to store in the wooden bins. He put lime over the potatoes. Lime looked like a white powder and was sprinkled over the potatoes to protect them from rotting during the winter.

Good "Vittles"

Mom knew how to stretch a dollar. She made cornmeal mush by cooking cornmeal, salt, and water together and then poured it in a bowl to chill overnight in the refrigerator. The next day she sliced it and fried it in an iron skillet of bacon grease. We liked to eat it with chunks of butter melting over the top. Some people liked to pour syrup over it, too.

We also had a lot of Mom's delicious homemade potato soup – after all, potatoes were our staple crop. She made fried potatoes, boiled potatoes, mashed potatoes – I never met a potato I didn't like. Often, a supper would consist of fried potatoes, cornbread made in a big iron skillet (when she flipped the cornbread out of the skillet, the underneath side had a nice light brown crust on it), and a pot of pinto beans that Mom had soaked overnight.

Pinto beans had to be cooked for several hours, but soaking them cut down on the cooking time. Sometimes, she'd switch from pinto beans, and cook the little white Navy beans, "soup beans," as we called them. Mom cooked them with plenty of water so we'd have "soup" to pour over our cornbread; these were my brother Joe's favorite (and Mom said he still cooks them for himself today, some fifty years later). Dad used to say that if I sat down at the supper table and didn't see any potatoes, I would say "there's nothing to eat." He said I even ate potatoes for dessert; if Mom had made a pie for supper, I'd have a piece of pie after my meal and then go back and eat a cold potato.

Dad brought home hamburger from the store about once a week. Mom would either make hamburgers for us (which I liked to eat with fresh corn on the cob in the summertime), or she would use it to make a meatloaf for Sunday dinners. Meatloaf, mashed potatoes, green beans, and biscuits or hot rolls, with a homemade layer cake for dessert, was a real treat for us. Mom always made Sunday dinners special.

Homemade Root Beer

Mom and Dad made root beer as a treat. They bought the root beer syrup at the drug store and mixed it in a big, stone jar with sugar, water and a little yeast to make it fizz. We saved our pop bottles when we bought soda pop from the store, and washed the bottles and refilled the bottles with our homemade root beer. Mom's sister gave her a bottle capper, and we could buy the caps to fit the bottles. My brothers and I helped fill the bottles, but I'm not sure just how much help we children really were, but it was exciting. Once the bottles were filled and capped, we had to lay the refilled containers on their sides, and just hope none blew a lid off! We had to wait two or three weeks to sample our homemade brew.

The New Bridge

One spring, when we were living at Munday and the torrential rains came, the creek overflowed its banks and the footbridge washed out. Dad borrowed a big, white horse from Uncle Virge. They went up on the hill behind our house, cut down trees, trimmed them up, hooked a chain on the logs, and the horse pulled them down the hill.

Dad and Mom built a bridge out of the logs and some old lumber. The bridge was made by placing two long logs across the creek; then boards were nailed across the logs, and steps were built on either end. Our first bridges didn't have hand railings, so we had to be very careful when crossing the creek.

In the meantime, we had to walk up to Orville and Etta Dewees's, on the other side of Grandma's, and cross their bridge until we built a new one.

Home Remedies

Orville and Etta — pronounced "Ettie" — was a couple who lived near Grandma Richard. They had been neighbors for years. Dad knew them when he was a boy.

Etta was a heavyset woman with dark hair that she wound up in a bun on the back of her head. Their wooden house had a front porch where you would often see Orville sitting and playing his French harp, otherwise known as the harmonica. Occasionally, Orville worked pumping oil wells. More often than not, it was said, he could be found sitting on the front porch. Etta was often hoeing in her garden or working in her flowers.

Etta had an old organ Dad enjoyed playing when he was a boy. He didn't really know anything about playing an organ, but he would play and have Etta guess the songs. She sat and listened to him for hours. She would guess a song, and he would say, "No, that's not it. Guess again." She had the most patience with him.

Sometimes Etta made homemade chocolate pudding for Dad. Grandma Richard didn't like chocolate, so he probably didn't get chocolate pudding at home.

Dad liked to sneak up on Etta and her sister Dora when they were washing clothes outside on the washboard. He would creep up behind them and yell, scaring them, causing the clothes to fly from their hands, landing on the ground. He thought it was such a good joke. Later, when he grew up, he asked Etta, "How did you ever stand me?"

Just about everybody in the community went to Etta Dewees's when they were sick. She always knew what kind of home remedy to use. When Dad and his family were growing up, they depended on Etta. There weren't any doctors nearby, and they didn't have a way to get to them if there were. The isolation the hills brought preserved many traditions. Etta seemed to be born with the gift of knowing how to help people when they were sick.

Etta used to take Louise and the other children back on the hill behind their house and pick mountain teaberry and hickory nuts. Mountain teaberry was a shrub with shiny green aromatic leaves that were edible. Mountain teaberry leaves makes a fine herbal tea. The leaves yield wintergreen oil. The red berries are also edible. Hickory nuts drop in early autumn as soon as they were loosened by rain or frost; however, it is important that they got to them early because they are also a favorite of the squirrels.

When Dad was a child, he often fell off their front porch when he was playing, and when he did, he passed out. His sister, Louise, panicked because she wouldn't know what to do. Their mother would shout, "Go get Etta!"

Louise would take off running like a deer up the path to Etta's house. Etta came hustling back down the path to take care of him. She kept a cool compress on his forehead and stayed with him until he was out of danger. She had a way of calming not only her patients, but the other family members, too.

Once, my brother Joe had hives really bad. Etta had Mom boil red clover to make a tea for him. It worked.

Dad's Sisters

Dad's sister Lyla told me about the two-story house her family had before they built the one that I remember. In 1930, when Grandma Richard was two weeks away from delivering Lyla, their house caught on fire.

Their neighbor, Orville Dewees, saw the smoke and came running down the path. He didn't see two-year-old Denzil anywhere and asked frantically, "Where's Denzil? Where's Denzil?" Orville ran inside the blazing house to look for him. When he came back outside, he found Denzil safe, rolled up in a blanket.

In later years, Lyla pictured her mother and how she must have looked on that day – standing there on a crisp day in March – with only two weeks before her baby was to be born, looking at her home going up in flames. Lyla felt sad, thinking about what her mother went through. The family had to split up, staying with relatives temporarily until a new house could be built. Grandma Richard went to stay with her dad, Grandpa Pepper, a few miles away, where Lyla was born.

Dad's sister Louise told me about their Grandpa Harvey Richard and Grandma Emaline Richard, who lived with them in Munday. Grandma Emaline was a little slip of a woman. Louise didn't remember her ever getting angry in her life. Grandma Emaline would have my dad and his sister Lyla go with her up the hollow above Lula Wilson's to get rich dirt. There was no need for a compost pile; they had the dark, rich soil naturally at their fingertips. Louise especially remembered the pretty white lilies growing in that hollow. Dad and Lyla carried the dirt in buckets back to the house for their Grandma to plant flowers in. They didn't go out and buy flower pots back then. They were resourceful. Their grandma used any old pots and pans with little holes that ruined the container for cooking. She placed her petunias in the rich dirt, and had the banisters on the front porch lined with pretty pots of flowers.

There was a mulberry tree up the path, near Etta and Orville's. The mulberry looks similar to a blackberry, but is longer and skinnier. The berries are red when ripening, but turn dark purple to black when they fully ripen and are sweet. According to Louise, they ate the mulberries right off the tree. Mulberries can be used to make pies or tarts, but these berries probably never made it that far as long as the Richard children were around.

On Sunday afternoons, Etta and her sister Dora, would often take the children in the neighborhood back on the hill to pick mountain teaberries, or pick up hickory nuts in the fall. Louise remembered going with Etta and some of the children back on the hill behind her house one afternoon, while Dora took the rest of the children up the hollow behind her house. Ada was one of the little girls who went with Dora. Ada and her brothers, Russell and Jack, lived just a couple houses up from Dora's, at the mouth of the hollow at Straight Fork.

A copperhead bit Ada that afternoon, and when they got her out of the hollow, they took her to the hospital. She was a very sick little girl. Louise was traumatized by the incident. They pulled the sheet back and let Louise see her leg, which had been cut four or five inches to let the venom out. Ada survived.

Louise and her brothers and sisters went to Bell School at Munday when they were children. Gilla Davis was her teacher. She remembered Ms. Davis because she held her back one year, just because of her age; it had nothing to do with her grades. Louise was older than her brother Lester but they were less than a year apart. Ms. Davis held Louise back a year so she and her brother would be in the same grade the following year, and ultimately they graduated from high school together. Louise attended school with her neighbors, Ada, and her brothers, Russell and Jack. One day, Ms. Davis asked Russell a question by giving him some clues.

"What grows under the ground, is in a shell, and you can eat it?" Ms. Davis asked.

Russell couldn't speak very plain, but he pondered on it for a while and then replied, "Well, I can't 'itely (rightly) say."

Ms. Davis asked, "Well, Russell, could it be peanuts?"

Russell hesitated for just a moment, and then with all the confidence he could muster, he answered, "Oh, yeah. It's peanuts!" (Not having any idea what the answer was until Ms. Davis told him, Russell just wanted to let on like he did. He was about as mischievous as Tom Sawyer).

Although we didn't have any moonshiners in the family as far as I know, I've heard that there may have been some moonshine whiskey being made not too far from my dad's family's farm. Their neighbor Dora liked to sit out on her porch and swing for hours and watch the neighbors pass by, or just enjoy the evening air. The neighbor children, Ada, Russell, and Jack had to cross over her big footbridge to get to their house, at the mouth of the hollow. Late one evening, while Dora was in her porch swing, the two boys came across the bridge. She heard Russell ask Jack, "Did you get the 'hickey bottle? Did you get the 'hickey bottle?'"

Russell couldn't say whiskey very plain. Jack hushed Russell.

"Shh! Dora will hear you!"

Of course, Dora heard them, but didn't let on. The moonshine was probably being made right up the hollow from their house, right under their noses, but nobody let on like they knew anything.

Before the underpinning was put on the front of their house, and while Dad and Lyla were very young, they played under the porch. Dad played with his little cars. Their hen and her little biddies wandered under there one day when Lyla was just a little thing. She picked up a stick and popped one of the little biddies on the head and exclaimed, "Now, it's asleep." She didn't realize the sleep was permanent.

Louise remembered having only one baby doll when she was a little girl. One day, she was so excited because she was going to get to go play at her friend Hilda's house. Louise had her doll in her arms and was running through her yard at high speed; however, she forgot about her mom's clothesline being down over the bank; it caught her under the chin and threw her backward on the ground, knocking her out. Needless to say, she didn't get to play with Hilda that day.

Louise and some of her siblings went around to Hunter and Verba (pronounced "Verbie") Deweese's, which is past Aunt Esther's at Munday. They crossed their bridge and headed up the hollow past the house where they knew there was a patch of ground cedar. It looked similar to pine, but ground cedar grew on the ground, not on trees. They gathered the ground cedar and took it home. Louise made Christmas wreaths and hung them in their windows. Those were the only wreaths they ever had. She made pretty crepe paper bows for them too.

Louise enjoyed crafts and at Easter, made Easter baskets out of round oats boxes. She cut the box off about halfway and saved enough to make a bail, or handle. Crepe paper was glued all over the box for decoration. Louise also made roses and other flowers out of crepe paper; then dipped the flowers in paraffin wax so it would harden.

When they were growing up, there were nine of them in all sitting at the big long table, five children plus their mom and dad, and their Grandpa Harvey and Grandma Emaline. With a family that big, there were a lot of dishes and silverware to wash. Lyla had to wash dishes, which seemed like an enormous task when she looked at the kitchen sink after a family meal. She asked her little brother Arlis if he would dry the silverware one day and he replied, "Oh, no."

Lyla told him that if he did, she would play a game of Old Maid with him. He finally relented, and it didn't take him long to finish off the dishpan of silverware. Lyla remembered her brother was fast, even at an early age. When they were finished with the dishes, Arlis pulled out the deck of cards and said, "Let's play, but Lyla answered, "No, I was just kidding."

Arlis got so mad he picked up whatever he could get hold of and threw it at her. He had a terrible temper.

While Louise was in high school, she was writing in her tablet one night after supper but her dad thought she was doing her homework. He told Lyla to go ahead and wash the dishes. Louise was actually writing a letter to her boyfriend, Jack Mathess, instead. Lyla was so angry; Louise was writing a letter and she felt like she was the one being punished.

Christmas was a special time. Their presents under the tree were in big white boxes, the kind boots used to come in. The boxes were personalized with their names written with a red pencil. Lyla remembered getting material for a new dress one year. Some children today would be appalled at such a gift, but Lyla wasn't disappointed; she was excited instead. A new dress wasn't something they got every day.

They had candy and oranges at Christmas, and always English walnuts, which was a tradition my dad continued. We always had English walnuts under our tree. Lyla asked for an umbrella one Christmas. She knew her mom ordered from the mail-order catalog. But the umbrella didn't arrive, and her mom was very disappointed. The next year, Lyla asked for the umbrella again, and that time she got her wish. The little umbrella had a wooden block on the handle with a picture of a puppy dog, and when you opened it up, it had pictures of animals all over it. Even though it was about ten degrees below zero, and no sign of rain anytime soon, Lyla took her little umbrella outside; the umbrella in the severe cold weather made a cracking sound when she closed it up because it had frozen. She thought she had broken it, but she hadn't.

One Christmas, Louise received an embroidery kit. It had little cardboard hoops, a pair of scissors, three or four squares to embroidery, and a few colors of embroidery floss. Louise was so excited; she said she thought she had "died and gone to heaven."

Lyla wanted to go sleigh riding down the hill behind their house with her brother Lester. Her mom told her not to wear her blue coat if she was going out to play. The coat was a hand-me-down from one of her relatives, but it was practically like new. Lyla put on the little blue coat and ran outside and jumped on the sled with her brother. They went down the hill and under the barbwire fence, tearing the little coat all to pieces. Her mom was so angry.

When Louise was in high school, she often stayed with some of the families in the neighborhood to help them with their house cleaning and chores, and also to make a little money. She stayed with Ada Munday, who lived a couple houses past the Methodist church. She earned $1 a week in the winter, and $2 a week in the summer.

Louise also stayed with another couple in the community, Lonnie and Opal Davis, and helped them out for a while. Opal was in a wheelchair at the time.

Louise bought a shiny tea kettle with a copper bottom for their mom. They only had a dishpan to heat water in before that. Louise was away working in Clarksburg while Lyla was still at home. Lyla dropped the tea kettle one day and bent it. Her mom was so upset with her at first until Grandma Emaline reminded her, "You should be glad she didn't scald herself to death."

Her grandma was always taking up for her. Grandma Emaline told Lyla that no matter how many more children her parents might have, she would always love her. When Lyla was three years old, her brother Arlis was born. Grandma Emaline doted on little Arlis, too.

When Arlis was old enough to play with his trucks, he made a road for them in the bottom below the house. He didn't want his sister Lyla messing it up, so when she came down to where he was, he started throwing rocks at her, and she ran toward the house. Their dad heard about the rock throwing before, but hadn't caught Arlis in the act until that day. Arlis never got a spanking; his dad just scolded him.

Lyla remembered when Aunt Nina's boys, Ben and Bill, came over to visit. Arlis didn't get along with his cousins. One day, they were fighting about something and Grandma Richard switched all three of them. Arlis was so mad that he got some white material and cut it into strips; he wrapped himself all up in these bandages and went out and sat on the front porch, hoping people would go by and see him and feel sorry for him.

Their Grandma Emaline became sick in her later years, and it was difficult to give her the care she needed at home. The family asked if she could stay at Uncle Bob Davis' since they were the first to have an indoor bathroom. They agreed, if Louise would come along, too, and help her cousin Hilda. Uncle Bob lived just down the road, less than a mile away. Louise stayed with them and cared for her grandma until she passed away. Lyla said she felt as though her world would end when she lost her grandma.

Even after some seventy years passed, my aunts looked back fondly on their childhood, missing their parents and grandparents, knowing they didn't have a lot of material things when they were younger, yet thankful for what they did have, and for the love and qualities their family instilled in them. And now, as parents and grandparents themselves, they have endeavored to instill those same qualities in their children and grandchildren. They give love and receive love in return, not only from their immediate families, but also from their extended family and friends alike.

Trot Line

Dad had a boat he took to the river to set trot lines. Mom would go along and paddle the boat while Dad set the lines. He would get a heavy string and stretch it across the river, securing it on either side and letting the slack down so it would be hidden in the water, all but enough on either end so he could locate it.

He tied huge hooks on the line a few feet apart and baited them, looking to catch the big fish in the river. My brother Jay remembered going fishing along the creek bank and catching fish for Dad to use for bait on the trotline. They set the lines at night, using a lantern in the boat for light. They came back before daylight to check the lines. Dad caught several kinds of fish on the trotline – from bass, catfish (mud-cat and blue-cat), and pike.

Frog Gigging

Dad liked frog legs so he talked Mom into going frog gigging with him. They used the boat to get close to the riverbank where the frogs were. They "gigged" the frogs with a long handled spear-like thing called a "gig" and hauled them into the boat.

Dad cleaned the frogs and put the legs in a pot of salted water. I can still see those frog legs jumping in the pot on the kitchen sink. Mom said they were just quivering. Ugh!

Our neighbor fried them up for Dad to eat. Mom didn't want any part of it.

Canning Chickens

Growing up, we didn't have a big freezer to keep meat and such in, so we had to can a lot of our food. Dad got a good deal on a whole mess of live chickens in Elizabeth once. He brought them home for us to can, which was nearly a fiasco.

Dad killed the chickens while Mom kept a big aluminum tub of scalding water ready to douse them in; then, we plucked all the feathers off. The smell was horrible! They cut them up and sealed the chicken in quart jars.

Mom placed the jars in a large pressure canner and cooked them until she knew they would keep without spoiling. The jars were then stored in the cellar. We had chicken on hand at any time.

The River

My dad loved to camp and fish, and I remember one day in particular when we took my friend Susie with us. Susie lived just around the bend from Grandma Maze's.

Dad and Mom were fishing in the Little Kanawha when Susie and I decided to take a walk along the riverbank. About all I ever caught was sunfish anyway. It was such a nice, shady path to walk along the river under the tall trees. We were enjoying the day, talking about nothing in particular, when my foot slipped and I rolled over the bank into the deep water.

I bobbed up and down, gasping for air and yelling for help. Susie stood still at the top of the bank, as if paralyzed. Finally, she ran to get help. Dad heard our screams and came running. Sliding down over the bank, catching himself on tree roots or whatever he could get a hold of, he dived in after me. By that time, Mom was standing at the top of the riverbank, frozen with fear. I'm sure Dad must have been terrified, but when his fatherly instinct kicked in, all he could think of was saving me; fear for his own life hadn't crossed his mind.

I thought my parents had some nerve taking my picture when we got home – standing in the yard in my soaking-wet dress and stringy hair. Looking back now, I realize they were probably just thankful their daughter was home, alive.

On The Lake

Aunt Lyla and Uncle Joe lived in Nutter Fort, West Virginia, near Clarksburg. During my school holidays, they invited me to stay with them for a week in the summer, and made a special effort to see that I had a good time.

We went to Tygart Lake State Park which was just minutes from the historic town of Grafton, also known as the "Birthplace of Mother's Day." Aunt Lyla and Uncle Joe had a boat docked at the lake, and they took me boating and swimming with them. I felt really important when Uncle Joe let me steer his boat.

While we were out in the middle of the lake, Aunt Lyla jumped over the side into the deep water. She was a good swimmer, and braver than I. I would have been terrified to jump in the water at that depth. Borrowing one of her bathing suits, I played it safe and ventured into the water only when we had docked near the shore.

When we got back to the house, Uncle Joe decided to grill hamburgers. I remember the tall mouth-watering burgers he pulled off the grill. Aunt Lyla was also a good cook, and we enjoyed sharing recipes.

My aunt and I both enjoyed clothes, and she usually took me shopping at the mall when I went to visit in the summer. Often times before I returned home, she would share some of her pretty clothes with me. I loved going in her bedroom, watching her open the closet door, seeing all the clothes hanging there which you could tell didn't come from a discount store. One blouse in particular that I thought was beautiful was a deep green and black striped satin blouse. I believe Mom was almost as excited to see the expensive clothes and shoes that I brought home as I was to receive them. This was a special time that my aunt and I shared together. I was very fortunate to have these summers to remember.

The Goodnights

A little ways past Grandma Richard's house, and on beyond Etta & Orville's, was a little white house where Etta's sister, Dora, lived. I remember

Wanda Goodnight, Dora's daughter-in-law. Wanda sometimes went with us to the country store over at Industry, about three or four miles away. It was an old store with wooden floors and big barrels setting near the counter. Candy jars with appealing goodies lined the counter and caught our attention. I remember Wanda bought us a sack of caramel creams once – soft, chewy caramels with the white centers. They were so good.

Just below the store was a dirt road that wound down around the river. Sometimes, Dad took us camping and fishing down there. Further down that road at Table Rock, legend has it that at night when you hear a loud noise, like a chain saw coming across the water, it's the ghost that haunts that part of the river. I never cared to go down as far as Table Rock, and certainly not at night.

Santa on the Roof

Christmas was always a magical time for us. Dad loved Christmas and he and Mom always made a great effort to make it special. Dad took me in the woods to cut down the Christmas tree. We'd brave the cold weather and the snow. One year, I was so cold when we got back to the house I told Mom I wasn't going back outside until July.

Our Christmas gifts were wrapped in white tissue paper, then our names were written on them with glue and sprinkled with red glitter. This created sparkling, personalized packages for each of us.

One Christmas Eve, Dad was very excited and said to us, "Listen. I think I hear sleigh bells." We all got quiet as a mouse; so quiet in fact, we thought we heard them, too! Then Dad opened the door – and sure enough, there on our enclosed porch, were packages from "Santa."

I remember a doll I got for Christmas one year. She was tall with blond hair and long, dark eyelashes. She wore the prettiest, bright blue dress. I could hold her hands, and with my help, she could walk to me. Once, Santa brought me a baby buggy for my dolls. My buggy wasn't like typical strollers; mine looked like a bassinet on wheels. I could put my dolls in the buggy and walk them down through the bottom when the weather was warmer.

I remember Joe getting a football one year and Jay got a sled. We loved to go sleigh riding. We'd go out and get all cold and wet in the snow, and then we'd come inside to get warm. We took off our coats and gloves and laid them in front of the gas stove to dry out, then we'd go back outside and sleigh ride again.

The "Truth" About Santa Claus

As a youngster sitting on the front pew of the little Methodist church with my red-headed cousins, Mark and Becky, a few weeks before Christmas, it seemed like any other Sunday until Mark broke the news to me – there was no Santa Claus. I was shocked with disbelief, and argued with every fiber of my being that *there was so* a Santa Claus! After all, he had brought us presents all these years. And what about the sleigh bells I heard when Dad told us to listen, and we all heard them – the presents were on the porch when he opened the door! Mark insisted that was just a story.

How could something I'd believed in all these years be just a story? We went to Sunday school with Grandma Richard, so Dad and Mom were not there for me to question them about it, but just as soon as I got home, I told Mom about Mark's claim. I pleaded with her to tell me that what he said was not true, but she just looked at me with such sadness in her eyes. At that moment, my hopes were shattered and my little heart was broken.

Reunions and Celebrations

Bell School was the meeting place for family reunions and birthday celebrations for many years. The Richard Reunion was held there for several years. Members of the Richard family took turns coordinating the event. The coordinator made sure invitations were sent out, and that the gifts were purchased for door prizes and special prizes, such as for the oldest relative there. Grandma Richard usually got the prize for being the oldest relative, having been born June 9, 1900. I was the coordinator for our family one year, and I picked out a pretty lamp for the prize for the oldest relative. Grandma was happy with it, and I think she would have been very disappointed if she hadn't won. Each family brought food, and we put it all out together to have a big, picnic-type meal. Later, we played games and awarded prizes. I guess being at the old schoolhouse brought back a lot of memories for Dad and his sisters, Lyla and Louise. Dad was a cut-up, and sometimes he would pretend they were still in school. He chased them with the chalkboard erasers, and Aunt Lyla pretended she was teaching.

We celebrated Grandma Richard's 80th birthday at Bell School with a special cake Aunt Lyla made for the occasion, and we had a nice time celebrating the landmark birthday with Grandma.

On Memorial Day weekends, Grandma Richard's family, on the Pepper side, met at Bell School and had a picnic lunch, and then went to Wolverton Cemetery, the family graveyard, to place flowers on the graves of our family members. For several years, until the road was graveled, we had to park the cars at the foot of the hill, and then walk up to the cemetery because the road was not passable. Among those who came for these Memorial Day weekends were Grandma's brothers and their wives, Grandma's sisters Nina and

Thelma, and Thelma's husband, Jess, Grandma's children, including Denzil, Lyla her husband, Joe, and their son, Jimmy, along with Joe's mother, Mrs. Kopshina, My dad and our family. Louise lived a long way off and didn't usually get to come.

These family get-togethers were very laid-back; no one tried to compete with other family members, a lot of love and happiness brought us together year after year. My dad looked so forward to these family get-togethers. I have kept several photos of our family gatherings at Bell School.

The Norwegian Elkhound

Wayne Toney lived across from Shimer's store in Munday. His Norwegian elkhound had a litter of puppies. They were the cutest little balls of fur you could imagine, or at least my brother Joe thought so. Wayne didn't really want to part with any of the puppies, and especially not the one Joe picked out, but when Dad offered him $10, he finally relented.

These dogs are known to be loyal, intelligent companions, but I doubt that Joe was worried about the dog being loyal or intelligent at the time, he did want a companion, however, and he named his pup Tuck.

Tuck was gray and black with a lighter underside. His nose and pointed ears were black. He grew to be a hardy, medium-sized dog, sturdy and squarely built. His tail was curled and rolled tightly over his back. His eyes were dark brown with a friendly expression, and sometimes we thought he smiled. He could be somewhat reserved with strangers, but eager to greet us, especially when we came home from school in the afternoons. We had Tuck with us for about a year while we were living in Munday, and then took him with us when we moved out on Ambler Ridge and then to Walton in Roane County.

Mom took Tuck to Joe Cain's Veterinarian Clinic at Spencer when it was time to get his vaccinations. We had known our vet for years. He lived in Calhoun County, and his main clinic was beside his house near Big Bend. After we moved to Walton, we were glad to find out that he had built a clinic on the outskirts of Spencer, the county seat, because it was closer for us.

One year, when we took Tuck to Spencer for his vaccinations, Mom had him on a leash, and Joe Cain asked her, "Who's leading who?" Tuck was strong, and could almost pull Mom around. Joe Cain had always had a sense of humor. I remember one time while we were living at Walton, my cat, Misty, got real sick in the middle of the night, and we called the vet at his home. He told us to go ahead and bring the cat to the clinic in Calhoun County. It was a long drive, and I was so worried about her. When we got there, he said to me in a gentle voice, "I don't know which one of you looks the worst." My cat had inner ear trouble and her eyes were rolling from side to side, and she was sick at her stomach. I guess I didn't look much better. He was in the right business, because he really had compassion for animals.

Tuck had the stamina to hunt all day long, and he was a good squirrel dog. My dad and brothers liked to hunt, not Joe so much, but Jay really enjoyed it, and Tuck loved being in the woods and roaming through the hills. Dad took him to work with him sometimes as he worked outside in the oil fields. Tuck would stay around the wells with him, or sometimes wander off and hunt.

When Tuck got older, he became sick and couldn't get around very well. I can remember him laying on a rug in the utility room with the saddest brown eyes looking up at us. We did everything we could for him, and tried to make him as comfortable as possible. Tuck had swollen places on his body, like knots, and I didn't know what they were at the time; looking back now,

I think they must have been tumors. Dad said that when Tuck looked up at him with those sad brown eyes, it was as if he was saying, "Can't you help me?"

When he died, we buried him in the pet cemetery in the woods above our house where our other pets were buried. Dad made headstones out of cement for our pets, and carved their names in the cement.

"Batching It"

Dad worked for Pennzoil while we were living beside Grandma in Munday. He and some of his friends transferred to Walton in Roane County, which was about an hour and a half away.

They rented a house in Walton – they called it a shanty – and were "batching it" away from home. They lived in their shanty during the work week and went home to their families for the weekend. They had separate household chores to do. My dad was the main cook, and if anybody complained, they got the job.

Eventually, Dad found a house to buy for us about a mile out of Walton. It was a two-story, white farmhouse that needed repairs, but Dad was handy around the house, and wasn't afraid of hard work. We rented a house on Ambler Ridge, and then spent a few months back in Munday, while Dad got our new house at Walton ready.

Ambler Ridge

When I was about 11, before we moved to Walton, Dad rented the house on Ambler Ridge, a few miles from Walton. It had a hand pump on the sink in the kitchen. It pumped the water in from a cistern outside. Water ran off the house and down into that reservoir.

Grandma hated for us to leave Munday, and we were very sad, but Dad's job was in Walton. It was important that we all be together as a family. Uncle Denzil brought Grandma to visit us. I don't think I would have been able to bear it otherwise.

Joe was old enough to go to school at Walton High, but Jay and I were younger and had to attend the one-room schoolhouse on Ambler Ridge. It was actually a two-room schoolhouse, but one room was for storage. Ms. Painter was our teacher. She lived past our house out the ridge.

Jay was always getting into trouble at school. I think he spent more time standing in the corner than sitting at his desk. It reminds me now of Willie Olsen in *Little House on the Prairie*; he was always standing in the corner in that schoolhouse.

Berneice was in my class. She had long, brown hair that she curled in long spirals on either side of her face, and pinned them back out of her eyes with bobby pins. One day she said something funny and I got so tickled I couldn't stop giggling. Ms. Painter made me stand in the corner. I was never so humiliated in all my young life.

I remember a record player in the spare room of the school. We were allowed to bring records and play music at recess. One day, I brought my 45-rpm record of Elvis Presley's "Return to Sender." We played that record over and over until it nearly drove Ms. Painter crazy.

"...Return to sender, address unknown
No such number, no such home
We had a quarrel, a lover's spat
I write I'm sorry, but my letter keeps coming back..."

With the beginning of fall, came the big thick Sears catalog in the mail, our wish book, as we called it. Dad always teased me about how much I loved looking through that catalog, and how I'd wear out the pages before Christmas arrived. Even as I got older, Dad teased me and told me he was going to get me a wish book as my Christmas present.

Dad took me to cut down our Christmas tree in December the year we lived on Ambler Ridge. I still have a picture of us standing out in the yard in the snow with our Christmas tree. We had always been with Grandma Richard and Denzil at Christmastime, so Denzil brought Grandma to Ambler Ridge. However, I came down with the flu or something like it, and I didn't get to enjoy their visit.

Hermie was a neighbor who lived across the road from our house, up on the bank. I thought Hermie was an unusual name for a woman. She was rather modest looking, with shoulder length, wavy hair with a touch of gray in it. I was at her house one day when some of her friends visited. The women wore short dresses, and one of them had on those tall, white boots that came just below the knee and zipped up the side. The women laughed and talked while songs were playing on the radio in the background like Jeanie C. Riley's "Harper Valley PTA."

"... Well the note said Mrs. Johnson you're wearing your dresses way too high
It's reported you've been drinkin' and a runnin' round with men and goin' wild
And we don't believe you oughta be a bringin' up your little girl this way
And it was signed by the secretary Harper Valley PTA..."

I caught Hermie's eye as she looked at me and smiled, noticing my uneasiness in this crowd. I was an eleven-year-old with no worldly experience. Nor was I ready for any.

Chapter 5
A New Home: Walton

Moving Day

Moving day finally arrived. We left Munday and moved to Walton. It was only about an hour and a half from Grandma's house, but it seemed like the end of the earth. I was very sad to leave her and my school friends behind.

We moved into a two-story, old, white farmhouse. My bedroom was upstairs, over the kitchen.

The orange moving van backed up to the front porch and the movers unloaded all of our possessions. I didn't know until later we had a "spy" across the road. The little girl who lived over there with her parents was my age and we soon became great friends.

On moving day, Janet was so curious to see who her new neighbors were that she climbed up on the banister on her front porch, but she couldn't tell what the people across the road looked like. So, she climbed up the tree in front of the house and rested on a limb to get a "bird's-eye-view" of what was going on next door, and get a glimpse of what would eventually change her life as she knew it.

Janet was slender with long, wavy, dark blond hair. She and I became great friends from the moment we met. We were inseparable. She was the sister I never had. We were truly kindred spirits, just like Anne and Diana in *Anne of Green Gables*.

It was easy to fall in love with her parents. Janet's dad, Harry, and her mom, Levie, were wonderful people, and became a second family to me.

They were always insisting I have something to eat when I came over to see Janet. They worked hard, raised a garden, and did a lot of canning. They were down-to-earth people, some of the best you could find.

I remember one time Harry was over at our house visiting. We were sitting in the backyard under some shade trees. A bird plopped a nice, big "present" down on my head. I was so embarrassed. Harry got so tickled, and with his dry sense of humor, he said to me, "They sing for some people."

One year for Christmas, while I was still living at home, Dad and Mom gave me a set of stainless steel cookware, and Janet's parents gave her a set of dishes. When I showed my present to Harry, he said, "Even old maids have to eat." Of course, neither Janet nor I was an old maid, but he loved to tease us.

Farmhouse

The farmhouse we moved into was originally Janet's family home when it was built way back over the hill from where it's now located. Of course, at that time, the house was in much better condition and had an L-shape addition. Janet took me for a walk over the hill and showed me the land where their house was when she was a little girl.

We were told the story of how it was moved to its new location. When the house was moved from over the hill, they bolted an enormous board under the house to stabilize it. The brakes went out on the truck during the move, but amazingly enough, the gaslights and fixtures on the house weren't broken. Once the house was moved, the porches were re-attached, but the L-shape addition was not. The house had been rented out before Dad bought it, and it was in much poorer shape than when Janet and her family lived in it.

Handy Man & Woman

Our dad had our house in Walton remodeled, and he did a lot of the work himself. He was even brave enough to climb up the tall ladder and paint our steep tin roof. I loved to hear it rain on that roof as it could lull you to sleep.

We didn't have a water well when we first moved to Walton. The only water we had was spring water, which ran through a pipe from up the hollow, but there was very little water pressure. In the summertime, when the weather was hot and dry, we hardly got any water through the lines. We had no bathroom, no running water – only in the kitchen sink, and that was limited. Dad had to have a well drilled. The driller lived on the other side of Left Hand Hill, a few miles from us. He drove a school bus during the day, but had a drilling rig and drilled wells on the side.

Once we had the well drilled, Dad enclosed part of the back porch, along with Mom's help, and made it into a utility room for the clothes washer and dryer, and a small bathroom. Before that, we had an outhouse which was a "two-seater," the first I had ever seen, and Joe thought we were really coming up in the world compared to the "one-seater" we had in Munday. Joe was upset when the outhouse was torn down after the bathroom was added on.

Prior to our new bathroom, we had to heat water on the stove and carry it upstairs to take a "sponge bath." But when the utility room was enclosed, and before the bathroom was finished, we had a round, galvanized tub we could actually sit in and take a bath; this required a lot of water being heated on the stove and carried into the utility room.

This first water well was certainly an improvement over the spring water, but the well wasn't very deep, and that limited how much water we used in a day. Mom remembered that she could only wash one load of clothes a day, unless it rained a lot, then she could wait till evening and run another load. With a husband who worked in the oil fields and three growing children, there were plenty of dirty clothes to wash.

After several years, that well caved in, and we had to have another one drilled. The second well was drilled deeper and produced more water, so Mom wasn't as limited on the amount of wash she could do in a day, and we could take showers, a new luxury for us.

The farmhouse didn't have central heat and air, so we used fans to cool the house in the summer, and we eventually put in a couple of air conditioning window units downstairs. To heat the house, we had a gas burning stove in the living room and a smaller one in the bathroom. When the weather was really cold, we turned on the gas burners on the kitchen stove, too.

Dad built a cement block cellar in the backyard to store our canned goods and potatoes in, and he built a building over top for storage. I loved to go barefoot, and step into the cellar on the cool, cement floor. It was a quick way to get cooled off on a hot summer day.

Mom planted flowers on either side of the front steps, and made a flower garden along the hillside to the left of the house. She had a beautiful Snowball bush below the house, which bloomed in late spring; it had flower clusters, or snowballs, sometimes up to eight inches wide. The Cleome, or spider flower, is known for its very long seedpods. They develop at the bottom of the flowers on the stalk and give the plants a spidery look. The flowers perch atop stems that grow as high as an adult's head. Mom brought these lovely, pink flowers from our house at Munday.

In the backyard, Dad built a barbecue pit out of cement blocks, and he also built a picnic table with benches that went all the way around a big tree.

I think Dad knew how to do just about anything. He was a very hard worker, and learned at an early age to be independent as his ancestors were before him, learning the ways of providing for your family, whether it was putting a roof over our heads or planting and harvesting the crops. We had a lot of good times in our backyard, sitting around that tree and cooking out with family and friends. Sometimes my grandmothers would come down and enjoy it with us, and sometimes Aunt Louise or Aunt Lyla would visit.

During one of Aunt Lyla's visits, we went upstairs in my bedroom to listen to the radio. We had the music turned up, and we were dancing to it. We could feel the floor of that old house shake, but didn't think much about it until Dad started up the stairs, and in a very kind voice said to us, "You kids are making the lights shake down here." We decided to take it easy after that. We didn't want to go through the ceiling.

Antiques

When I was growing up, perhaps in my teens and into my early twenties, I wondered why my dad and his sister Lyla were so fascinated with old things.

I remember once when we visited Aunt Lyla and Uncle Joe at their home in Nutter Fort, and how excited Aunt Lyla was to show my dad some antiques she'd acquired. One thing in particular was a set of old-fashioned sleigh bells that she had hanging on her wall in the entryway, near the stairs which led up to the main part of the house. She also had some old irons, the kind they heated on the stove years ago when they ironed their clothes the old-fashioned way. An old telephone, in a wooden box, hung on the wall. To see them together, you would have thought Aunt Lyla and Dad had discovered buried treasure.

Dad collected treasures of his own. He had old tools, a washboard, and a big, iron dinner bell he hung on a tall pole which he had cemented in our backyard at Walton. He liked old bottles and jars, and sometimes dug for these treasures after he had torn down an old house, for the lumber it provided. I still have a blue transparent Mason jar of his that has "Mason Patent Nov. 30, 1858" on the front; it has the zinc lid with it. Dad and Mom both liked Depression glassware, and there were so many patterns and colors to choose from: the greens, pinks, cobalt blues, milk glass, and so many more. At one time, they had collected several pieces, but unfortunately, after time, some of it had to be sold. Mom's favorite was the pink glass, especially the Cabbage Rose and Cherry Blossom designs. We still have a few pieces of her mother's pink glassware, and a transparent green cake plate that was given to her as a gift.

Now, I have favorites of my own. I love to stop at a flea market or step into an antique shop and browse through the aisles of antique furniture, paintings and books. I especially enjoy finding antique kitchenware – old rolling pins, utensils, mixing bowls, pitchers, reamers (better known as juicers), glass refrigerator containers (now widely replaced by Rubbermaid or disposable plastic containers), butter dishes, salt and pepper shakers, and many other collectibles. Green Jadeite and transparent green are my favorite types of glass.

Grandma Richard had a light green Jadeite towel rack in her kitchen, and a green Jadeite mixing bowl. I have two pretty glasses that belonged to my Great-Grandpa Pepper; one has white dogwood blossoms, and the other has red tulips; peanut butter used to come in these glasses years ago. Mom bought me a set of green Jadeite salt and pepper shakers which I still have; I also have a dark brown Lysol bottle, some cobalt blue Milk of Magnesia bottles and some other bottles which may have held medicines; I have a clear glass jar-filler like they used in canning season, some green dinner plates which were a gift from a dear friend, a Sunnybrook egg carton dated 1934, a Sour Apples Bubble Gum box dated 1957 (the year I was born), a tin measuring cup and set of measuring spoons that look like they might have come over on the Mayflower, and a metal Chase & Sanborn coffee can with "Percolator Method Directions for Brewing Delicious Coffee" printed on the side.

Now that I'm older, I understand why my parents and Aunt Lyla enjoyed their antiques so much. It was like holding on to a small piece of their past, the enjoyable days of childhood when they grew up in a simpler time, a time to remember and hold dear.

Mountain Crafts & Quilting Bees

Grandma Richard and Grandma Maze were known for their beautiful homemade quilts in a variety of patterns. Grandma Maze also made comforters, which were heavier than quilts. She sewed comforters in patterns such as the nine-patch, using nine squares of material for each block, often postage stamp size, which was a good way to use up scraps of material left over from making dresses, skirts or jackets. The crazy-top was another design which was material sewn in several different directions, and was sewn together by hand, using a buttonhole stitch. Grandma went to the yard goods outlet store and bought large pieces of soft flannel or stretchy jersey for the back side of her comforters, and filled it with a roll of batten. These heavy comforters felt cozy on a cold winter's night; hence, the name comforter.

Some of the quilt patterns Grandma Richard and Grandma Maze used were the bowtie, double wedding ring, log cabin, ships, nine-patch, as well as appliquéd patterns such as the rose, butterfly, little Dutch girl, and little boy with a fishing pole. Once the quilts were pieced together or appliquéd, they were filled with a thinner batten than the comforters, and bleached muslin was sewn on the backside. Then they were stretched onto quilting frames. They fastened the quilt to each end of the frame; when one section was completed, the quilt could be rolled presenting a new section to be quilted, which was done with delicate hand stitches. Quilting was usually done in the winter, after the harvest and canning season was over. Sometimes, families got together and had quilting bees, helping one another out. Women could share family news, as well as exchange recipes, give and receive tips on raising children, and all in support of one another.

Mom remembered when my brothers got their bunk beds. They didn't have comforters to fit the new beds, and Mom's Grandma Rose invited her down to her house and the family made comforters for the boys.

Mom crocheted delicate lace doilies when they were popular back in the 1950s and 1960s. They were used to decorate the tops of furniture such as tables and dressers. Mom also quilted at home, but she didn't have a big quilting frame; she used very large quilting hoops made out of thin wood. She also crocheted, making potholders and house shoes for Christmas gifts.

An ideal way to view the many mountain crafts and traditions in the hills of West Virginia is to visit the Mountain State Arts & Craft Fair, which is held every summer at Cedar Lakes, Ripley, West Virginia, about twenty five miles from Spencer. We visited the Arts & Craft Fair after we moved to Walton, and I would recommend it to anyone living in, or visiting, the Mountain State who would like to get an overall view of mountain living, music, food, and storytelling. There was something for everyone in the family from taking a covered wagon ride, watching a blacksmith at work or watching a sheep shearing demonstration, which had the children enthralled. You could see anything from a handmade quilt show to traditional spinning wheels and blowing art glass. There was also cornmeal grinding, lye soap making, and apple butter cooking in a large kettle over an open fire. We could listen to storytelling of local folklore or watch a craftsman shape hardwoods into family heirlooms, and any number of other crafts. We could sit under a shade tree or on a hay bale and tap our feet to gospel, traditional Bluegrass, or other folk music. As well as the opportunity of taking home some of the homemade apple butter or a bag of fresh ground cornmeal, there were plenty of food booths set up to enjoy from morning till night. There were the traditional hotdogs or corndogs for the kids. Buckwheat cakes were served in the morning, and fried green tomato sandwiches and roasted ears of corn later in the day, as well as the traditional beans and cornbread. Apple dumplings or blackberry cobbler with homemade ice cream for dessert was a perfect way to top off the meal.

Dad's Ingenious Ways

Dad seemed to have a special aptitude for discovering ways to make extra money, or save money on projects.

Dad knew how to go into the woods and find ginseng, or "seng" as it was known in the Mountain State. Perhaps he had learned this from Etta Dewees when he was a little boy, when she took the children into the woods to look for plants, herbs, and nuts. Ginseng grows in rich soils in cool woods. They bear three to five large leaves with a few small, greenish-white flowers which grow on a short stalk from the center of the leaves, and appear in mid-spring until mid-summer. The fruit is a cluster of bright red berries, and is not to be confused with the red baneberry plant whose leaves are similar and also has a cluster of red berries; however, every part of the red baneberry plant, including the berries, is poisonous. Nor should it be confused with the

Virginia creeper, which also has five leaves (rarely three leaves); this plant has small, greenish flowers in late spring to small purplish-black berries in the fall; the berries are poisonous to humans, but are an important source of food for birds in the winter.

Dad dug the Ginseng root in the fall after the berries or seeds had fallen away. He sold it for a few hundred dollars a pound, but it took a lot of ginseng to make a pound. Ginseng was used to make medicines and dietary supplements.

Dad also tore down old houses to retrieve the lumber; the cost was usually just hauling it away. He used the wood and tin from these houses to build projects, like our cellar building. On his locations in the oil field, when the wooden tanks that held water were worn out and needed to be destroyed, he tore them down and brought the wood home. Mom remembered that he used the wood from one of these water tanks to build our footbridge over the little run out back when we lived at Walton. We crossed the footbridge to get from our backyard to our garden.

Dad also knew how to buy and sell. He seemed to have a knack for it. Sometimes he and Mom would go to auctions and buy up a large supply of tools or some other item of interest. He knew how to bid on them at a good price, and then he would resell the items at a reasonable price, which made the buyer feel as if he, too, had received a bargain in the process.

Under the Sheets

Grandma Maze and Aunt Louise both came to visit us at the same time one week when we lived in Walton. Grandma and Aunt Louise always got along really well, and we had a good time laughing, visiting and shopping together.

Mom gave them Joe's room to sleep in as he was away in the Navy. Grandma had gone to bed after Aunt Louise one night, getting undressed in the dark so not to wake her. No one realized until the next morning that Grandma had crawled in under both sheets and was lying on the bare mattress; they were really separated in the night. Everyone got the biggest laugh out of that. Sometimes the things "unplanned" are the most hilarious.

Oil Fields

When people think of West Virginia, they often think of coal. However, as the use of machinery grew in America, the demand for crude oil increased as this choice lubricant kept machines running smoothly. Legacy has it that soon after the birth of West Virginia many of its towns became covered with oil pumps and derricks. The Oil & Gas Museum was established in Parkersburg, and I understand that many of the old oil pumps were salvaged and on display at the museum.

My dad worked for Pennzoil in the oil fields. He had to keep the pumpjacks running. He also worked for another oil company part-time, several evenings a week. Some "pumping jacks" had electric starters and some had cranks you had to turn round and round as fast as you could to get them started. The oil was pumped out of the ground and ran through lines into big storage tanks, which were often located at the bottom of a hill. Dad had a long stick that he used to check the tanks to see if they were full enough for it to be shipped out. He also had to keep his locations mowed with a mowing scythe – that was hard work.

He took me to work with him one day, and I remember it was cold. There was a little shanty built out of tin that I stayed in which kept me sheltered from the wind. Dad brought his lunch pail with him, as Mom always packed him a good lunch, which usually included a piece of homemade pie in one of those Tupperware containers that's shaped just like a piece of pie, and a big thermos of coffee. He poured me a cup of coffee, and I dunked my cookies in it, but I couldn't drink it straight, as I didn't care for the strong taste.

Free Natural Gas

While living at Walton, we received free natural gas for several years. I was too young at the time to know about it, but that was part of the agreement when Dad bought our house. There were nine wells on that large farm (we had about an acre of that land) and the previous owner agreed to our having free gas. His farm consisted of several acres of woods, meadows, and dirt roads which we were allowed to explore as much as we liked.

We used the gas for heating the house, for cooking, for heating the water tank – we depended on it for everything.

In the really cold months of winter, the gas lines began to collect fluid and freeze off. We would wake up in the middle of the night and our house would be freezing. Dad and Mom would get up, get dressed in their warmest clothes and boots, and go out in temperatures ranging sometimes between 10 and 20 below zero. They walked the line to find where it was frozen, often trudging through very deep snow, and then they took the connections apart and got the line thawed out. Mom remembered it being treacherous and very difficult in the frigid temperatures.

The Samples

Howard and Mary Samples and their family lived in Walton, about a mile from us. They had two daughters, Brenda and Robin, and a little boy,

Sam. Mary also had an older son named Roger Miller, who was by her first husband. Roger's dad had passed away.

Howard and Dad soon became friends; they both worked for Pennzoil, pumping oil wells, out on Ambler Ridge. We also became friends with the rest of the family. I remember Brenda and Robin both played basketball in school, and Sam was the cutest little boy, with a smile that was infectious. As Brenda was the oldest of the girls, and closer to my age, I spent more time with her. Roger was about Joe's age, and they became good friends. They went to school together, joined the same Boy Scout troop and spent time playing basketball and camping out. Mom and Mary enjoyed each other's company. I remember Mary had the funniest laugh; she would get so tickled trying to tell us stories.

They were originally from Clay County, and after some time, Howard transferred back there. We still saw each other occasionally as we visited back and forth.

After high school, my brother Joe joined the Navy, and Roger was in the ministry and in education. I read in a September 15, 2005, article that "The State Board honored Roger Miller, the director of Student Services for Roane County Schools, by naming him the Paul J. Morris Character Educator of the Year." The Superintendent was quoted as saying this about Roger: "Mr. Miller not only teaches the six pillars [Trustworthiness, Respect, Responsibility, Fairness, Caring Attitude, and Good Citizenship], but lives them every day and instills their lessons in the students of Roane County."

I remember reading Joe's letters he wrote home to us from the Navy, and on several occasions, he asked about Roger, and inquired about his address because he wanted to stay in touch with him.

Chicken Pox - Share & Share Alike

My older brother, Joe, graduated from Walton High School on June 5, 1972, under the banner hailing their class motto, "The Future Is Ours: We Will Strive To Make It Better."

He had joined the Navy and was scheduled to leave for Great Lakes, Illinois the next day. However, he contracted chicken pox on graduation night, and his adventures of sailing on the high seas were delayed for a month, during which time he shared the pox with me.

The chicken pox started out as a rash of spots between the size of a pencil eraser and a dime. They were all over me, even on my face, in my ears, and in my hair. I was itching to death and wanted to scratch like a mangy dog. The blisters showed up in waves, so after some began to crust over, a new group would break out. Mom used pink Calamine lotion on us, which was supposed to help relieve the itching.

I was in the eighth grade when I got chicken pox (grades 7-12 were at the high school back then; we didn't have a middle school). I remember how embarrassed I was when my math teacher, Mr. Curtis Moore, teased me, "I thought chicken pox was just for children." He was sure surprised when I told him that my brother had gotten them on his graduation night. Joe might have thought "the future was his; and he was going to strive to make it better," but he had a delay in finding out if that was really true. In the meantime, I had several weeks of the *present* to endure.

Chapter 6

Hills, Hunting, and Homemade Ice Cream

Picking Persimmons & Wildflowers

Janet and I took long walks through the woods. We were walking up the dirt road behind our house one day as we climbed higher and higher up the hill, winding around until we came to a flat. It was much easier walking then. We came around a curve in the road and upon a persimmon tree. The round yellow fruit on the tree looked good so we decided to give it a try. Wow! What a shock! It was so sour I told Janet it "turned my mouth wrong-side-out." We soon discovered the fruit is edible only when fully ripe, after it has turned a bright orange, almost red color, but are extremely bitter when unripe.

We loved to walk through the meadows and pick wildflowers, and once we made a West Virginia Flower Book. I still have mine. I used a tablet of white paper, so my flowers would show up against the plain background. The flowers are faded now, and the scotch tape has turned a dark brown, but they're still intact with their names written underneath each one: Blue Violet, Dandelion, Honey Locus, Sweet Williams, Honeysuckle, Red Clover, Solomon's Seal, White Larkspur, Purple Larkspur, White Clover, Daisy, Sweet Yellow Clover, Ferns, Stone Crop, May Apple, Pink Trillium, White Trillium, Wild Ginger, Dogwood, Bluets, Apple Blossom, White Violet, Wild Strawberry, Ground Ivy, Wild Geranium, Rue Anemone, Cinquefoils, Flea Banes, Blue Bells, Redbud, and Wild Iris.

Squirrel Hunting

In the fall of the year, during squirrel season, Dad loved to go hunting in the woods above our house. Squirrel was a staple food when Dad grew up, and later when we came along. Squirrel hunting is often the first hunting experience for youngsters new to a sport of hunting. Dad taught Jay how to hunt, and he loved the sport. You may spark a lively debate among seasoned squirrel hunters as whether a shotgun or a .22 rifle is the best for the sport. Dad had both a 12-gauge shotgun and a .22 rifle, but he started Jay out with a .410.

Squirrels love trees that produce nuts, so any mature hickory, oak, or beechnut can be a good place to find a group of squirrels. You can tell where a squirrel has been because they leave small pieces of shells and hulls all over the ground where they have been eating. Squirrels can often be on the move in early mornings and later in the evenings as they scurry to hoard away food for the winter ahead.

Dad was a good shot and often got his limit for the day. Sometimes he would share with neighbors who also liked squirrels but were unable to hunt, like Mr. Woodie Jett, who lived at the mouth of McKown's Creek.

Dad brought the squirrels home and skinned them in our backyard. Then, he put them in a pot of salted water to soak. When they had soaked clean, Mom cut them up in sections (much like you would a chicken), and boiled them until tender, saving the broth to make gravy. She rolled them in flour and fried them in a cast iron skillet. She cooked homegrown sweet potatoes, and fixed them along with the squirrels, biscuits and gravy. Dad and Jay regarded this meal as delectable table fare.

Mistletoe "Tree"

Once while out walking, Janet and I found a very tall tree with clumps of something green in the very top. It turned out to be mistletoe. We called it our "mistletoe tree," but it wasn't really. We thought it was so romantic to have found mistletoe in the woods.

Mistletoe is a small shrub with thick leaves and small, waxy, white berries. It was so high up in the tree we couldn't climb up to get it, so Dad had to shoot down some for Christmastime.

Playing School

Janet and I didn't have to have expensive games to play when we were younger. We created our own. We often played "school" in her cellar building – a nice room over their cellar. And what class would be complete without snacks? We went down to her mom's kitchen and packed a couple of bananas and some oatmeal cream cakes and took them back up with us. We cut them in little pieces and took turns serving to each other.

Chased by the Bull

Mom used to babysit a little boy named Alan. He was eleven months old when he first came to us. He was a cute, blond-haired, blue-eyed, little boy who cried for two days. He and his family lived in Walton, and his mother worked at a factory in Spencer, about fifteen miles away. After two days of crying, Mom wasn't sure what she was getting herself into, but Alan became like one of the family. He was with us for several years.

Janet and I took Alan with us on one of our walks one summer day. Going for walks in the hills and through the fields and creeks was our favorite pastime.

There were cattle in the field above our house. That day we also found out there was a bull that didn't like us intruding on his territory.

He took off running after us. I grabbed Alan by one hand and Janet grabbed him by the other hand and we took off running with him, his feet dangling in the air, never touching the ground until we made it home safely.

Alan's Other Escapades

We took Alan everywhere we went. He was just like a little brother. Mom took us shopping in Spencer, and he loved to get under the clothes racks and hide. We'd have to chase him out of those big, round clothes racks. As we spun the rack around, he would dart in and out, playing his version of hide and seek.

Alan liked to put my dad's work boots on and walk around the yard. The boots were about as big as he was. He looked so ridiculous, but adorable.

Janet and I were playing school upstairs in my room one day when Alan climbed up on the bed. He was just a little thing because I remember him wearing white cloth diapers. He wanted to play with us, but when something didn't go his way, he exclaimed, "Dood Dod!" He was trying to say "Good God!" but it didn't come out that way. We didn't teach him to say such things, but we couldn't help but get tickled at him.

Alan was very much afraid of two things: airplanes flying overhead and thunderstorms. The noises terrified him. Mom tried to console him by reassuring him over and over about the airplanes and finally convinced him that there was nothing to fear. The thunderstorms were a different story. Mom finally gave them a name he could remember; she called them "boom booms" and somehow that made it tolerable. When it would thunder and lightning, he would say in a much calmer tone, "there's a boom boom."

When Alan was little, he liked to pull a kitchen chair over to the stove and climb up on it to watch me make peanut butter fudge, which was my dad's favorite. I'd put a little bit of the hot mixture into a small bowl, and Alan and I would sample it as it cooled. One day while we were making candy, he asked me "Deb-wuh, do you hav-tuh put the peanuh buttuh in it?" Translated, that is "Deborah, do you have to put the peanut butter in it?" He loved the taste of the sweet butter, milk and sugar mixture better before I even added the peanut butter. This brings back good memories, and when I make peanut butter fudge today, over thirty-five years later, I still think of him.

Leeches

Janet and I were wading in the creek one day when I looked down and saw something on my leg. I first thought it was a leaf and tried to brush it off, but I couldn't loosen it.

I quickly realized that it was no leaf. I frantically screamed at her, "Get it off! Get if off!"

She tried, but she replied, "I can't." She told me later that I answered her, "Leave it on! Leave it on!" I can't imagine saying that, but I know she was telling the truth. I was hysterical, but Janet kept her wits about her. She picked up a small stick and held it up to my leg. That bloodsucking-freshwater leech attached itself to the stick and let me go – much to my relief!

The Abandoned House

Janet and I walked up the dirt road toward the freshwater spring and found an old abandoned house at the base of the hollow. There were hills on the other three sides surrounding it.

As young girls, we had a vivid imagination. The place held an aura of mystery about it. The house was void of windows or doors and the wood was gray from lack of paint over the years. We wrote mystery notes and folded the papers up and stuck them in a crack in the wall – a safe place until we returned on another day – or so we thought.

My older brother was in the Boy Scouts and little did we know their troop planned a campout for that weekend and were going to be in that hollow. Nor did we know they would take shelter in that old house from a coming storm.

They found our notes – much to their amusement – and to our horror, I might add. I found this out the following morning when Joe brought them by our house for hot chocolate.

I hid myself in my upstairs bedroom until I was sure all the troops had retreated.

The Whippoorwills

I loved to go for walks up the hollow and climb the hill back of the old abandoned house. There was a meadow on the top of that hill, and if we were lucky, we would see a deer and hear his snort, just before he disappeared into the woods. My brothers and I were walking in that hollow one day when we heard a scream like nothing we had ever heard before. It wasn't a human scream. It sounded like some kind of wildcat, and it was so loud that it echoed in that hollow as if it had been amplified. It didn't take us long to high-tail it out of there.

After a long day exploring the hills and woods, I liked to stretch out across my bed at night, when the moonlight streamed through my open window, and I knew I was safe in my room, and I'd listen to the whippoorwill up the hollow call to its mate...*whip-poor-will, whip-poor-will, whip-poor-will...*while the sweet scent of the pink honeysuckle drifted in on the night air.

Deep and Shallow Water

There was a small body of water that ran by our house and flowed into the creek below.

It began up the hollow, an overflow of the freshwater spring. We called it the "run" as it was only about six feet wide, and too small to be called a stream. It wound in and out around the fields and along the half mile of dirt road between our house and the mouth of the hollow. It was life to the purple Sweet Williams and other wildflowers which grew along it, and refreshment to the birds and wild animals – the squirrels, foxes, raccoons, groundhogs, rabbits, and deer, which lived along its banks or in the woods nearby.

One spring when we had very heavy rains, the creek in front of us overflowed its banks and backed up the run beside our house, which flooded our yard. Water was everywhere and it steadily rose until our vehicles were in danger of being swept away. This happened at night, and Mom and Dad had to wade through the water in the dark, with only flashlights and the light from the front porch to guide them. Dad hooked a chain to the car, which Mom was in, and pulled them with the pickup to higher ground. Mom was scared to death that they would be swept away in the swift water. She was remembering the great flood of the mid-1950s, when the Little Kanawha River had flooded Grandma Rose's house, and the only way to reach her was by boat.

Camping & Sightseeing

Holly River State Park in Webster County is a serene place to relax and enjoy the outdoors. Dad took us camping, and even though there were cabins available for rent, we were going to "rough it." We took a tent and set up our campsite. We were prepared with not only blankets and pillows, but with our individual air mattresses (the kind you float on when you're swimming) for comfortable sleep. Wouldn't you just know that if anyone's mattress had to leak, it would have to be mine? I woke up early in the morning – too early to get up – with a deflated mattress, and found to my further distress, that the tent was pitched on a big flat rock! Once I'd survived that first night of sleep – or lack of it – the next day's sightseeing helped make up for what I'd lost. There was a clear, peaceful stream flowing through the Park, and the rhododendrons, with their large pink blooms and deep green leaves, were beautiful that time of year.

Blackwater Falls State Park is located in Davis, West Virginia. The Falls are beautiful year round, but are especially spectacular in autumn. The multi-colored leaves are most impressive in a panoramic view of the densely forested gorge. Although a daily excursion to the falls is worth the trip, some may wish to take advantage of the accommodations of the lodge, cabins, or the camping facilities, and may enjoy any number of recreational activities that the area offers.

Hawks Nest State Park is located about an hour from Charleston, West Virginia. The Cliffside Trail starts at the lodge and winds around the cliffs to the Hawks Nest Overlook. The trail has some steep slopes, but is worth the view of the hills and valleys with the river below. I've been to Hawks Nest on several occasions, but never in the winter; however, I have seen a photograph of the Overlook blanketed with snow, and it is indeed a wondrous sight. There are other trails for those wishing a more challenging hike to one of the overlooks, and for the very adventurous, they offer an aerial tramway from the lodge to the marina below. I enjoyed the gift shop which sold souvenirs, and I especially enjoyed their maple-leaf-shaped candies.

Cass Scenic Railroad State Park is located in Cass, West Virginia. I've never seen the trains at Cass, but my parents and Jay have. I've only seen pictures of them, and they remind me of the train on the show *Dr. Quinn, Medicine Woman.* My family took a ride on one of these steam-driven locomotives. The railroad was originally built to climb steep grades and haul heavy loads of lumber from the woods to the mill. Thick, black smoke pours from the train's stack as it begins its journey up the mountain.

Fenton Glass

Fenton Art Glass is located in Williamstown, West Virginia, near Parkersburg and also near historic Marietta, Ohio. We went on a tour of Fenton, and were amazed at not only the gift shop's wide array of beautiful displays of handmade glass artistry, but also of the friendly tour guides who took us through the factory to see the skilled glassmakers at work, blowing the different designs and shapes right before our eyes. I was surprised they let us get so close to the craftsmen and the hot glass.

During the Depression years, the company made practical items, such as tableware and mixing bowls, but now, along with more than 100 employees, they create artistic glass that is cherished by Fenton collectors locally and around the world. We were able to visit the area where the artists worked, painting beautiful flowers and other various designs on the glassware.

White Sulphur Springs

Dad and Mom took us to visit White Sulphur Springs in Greenbrier County one summer. We were able to tour the grounds and get close enough to see the springs' impressive resort, The Greenbrier, with its lavishly landscaped grounds in the distance. The Greenbrier was a huge white resort, and it was so large it reminded me of The White House. Although I have only seen the outside of the resort, I can almost imagine the awe-inspiring interior which has undoubtedly attracted dignitaries over the years.

Jethro and Elly May

My brother, Joe, chose raising hogs for his FFA project one year while we were living at Walton. Dad and Joe built a hog pen, up the hill, beyond the cellar building. It was Joe's responsibility to feed the hogs and take care of them; otherwise, he would not receive a good grade.

I named the hogs Jethro and Elly May. You should never name something that you're going to have to eat later.

When butchering day came, I was very upset. I wrote on the calendar in the kitchen, "Jethro and Elly May Murdered Today." It was not a happy Thanksgiving Day for me.

Mom and Dad didn't believe in wasting much, if anything. After all, they were born in the 1930s during the Depression era when things weren't plentiful, and their families both taught them to not be wasteful.

I hated sausage, hated the smell of it. I can still remember Mom frying up those sausage patties and canning it in jars to have sausage through the winter months. And, the pickled pig feet in the brown crock! When you lifted the plate off the crock, the smell was rancid! I can still see the hog's head –

in the big, blue speckled canner in the utility room – just waiting until Mom had time to make mincemeat for pies.

The lard was rendered and used for baking and frying. The hams were cured and hung up in the cellar building. I never cared for tenderloin or pork chops either. How could I eat Jethro and Elly May?

Majorettes

Janet and I both had shiny, silver batons in high school. We may not have tried out for the majorettes, but we still had our own audience.

Her front yard was up on a bank that overlooked the road where we could see the cars below. We marched with our batons – twirling, tossing, and catching – not on the high school football field, but we had the passing traffic as our cheering section.

Early Teens

My early teens – maybe fourteen or fifteen – seem a little fuzzy, or maybe hazy is a better word. I try to forget a lot of what happened. I think some of it is blocked from my memory. My dad's drinking came to a head then. He kept a bottle of whiskey in a brown paper bag, setting on the floor between the refrigerator and the stove, right behind his chair at the kitchen table, and very accessible. No watered-down drinks for him; he drank the strong stuff.

My bedroom was upstairs over the kitchen, and I heard all the fighting and hollering. Looking at our two-story house from the front yard, my bedroom was the one upstairs to the far left, Jay's bedroom was in the middle, and Joe's room was on the far right. It seems like Mom and Dad did most of their arguing in the kitchen. I was afraid to stay up in my room, and afraid to come down.

Christmas for us was horrible that year, which was so unusual, and almost unbelievable. Dad had always made Christmas so special for us. Mom told me Dad always made sure we had presents at Christmas, even if he had to go out and borrow the money. I remember Dad picking up the plates from the supper table and throwing them through the middle room, which was their bedroom, into the living room, and the crashing sound as they landed in broken pieces under the Christmas tree.

Mom had enough. She threatened to leave him and take us with her. My brother Joe was older and could escape. He joined the Navy after high school, but Jay and I were still at home.

Dad sobered up enough to listen to what Mom had to say. She was not going to put her children in jeopardy any longer. He knew she was serious, so he checked himself into a hospital to get help. It wasn't easy on either of them, or us. We went to the hospital to see him, and he would beg her to bring him a drink. But eventually he quit drinking. I know all those bad times were just the whiskey talking; it wasn't him. It was like someone else living inside his body. I didn't know that man.

My dad lived about ten years after that, sober. I couldn't have asked for a better dad then. His ability to overcome adversity enabled him to persevere through some very rough times. He had always worked so hard, sometimes two jobs, providing for his family, and making sure that we knew we were cared for and loved.

I cherish all the early years, and those last ten years we had with him. He was such a good dad. He and I were very close. I enjoyed having my picture taken with him, and I have several I treasure. I could always go to him when I had a problem, or if I was upset about something. I knew he'd have the answer. He would have done anything for us. He was always so strong, and so wise in my eyes.

Teen Heartthrobs & Favorite Shows

While growing up, as many other teenage girls, I loved to buy teen magazines with the pull-out posters of celebrities like Donny Osmond and his brothers, and hang the posters on my bedroom walls. I played Donny's record, "Puppy Love" over and over until I almost wore it out.

Some of my other favorite stars were Elvis, David Cassidy and The Partridge Family, Chad Everett (*Medical Center*), Michael Landon and Pernell Roberts (both of *Bonanza*), Robert Redford, Paul Newman, Robert Urich, and last but certainly not least, Richard Thomas and anything to do with *The Waltons*. Along with magazine posters and articles, I sent away to Jeri of Hollywood, Hollywood, California for photos of my favorite stars. The walls of my room were plastered with these.

I watched *American Bandstand*, a television show that aired on Saturdays, and stood in front of our television and danced to the Top-40 style songs right along with the other teenagers on the show. I grew up learning dance steps from watching the show, and when I was older and had the chance to dance with partners (instead of just the television), I wasn't exactly a wallflower. I remember the show being hosted by Dick Clark (but it had a different host and a different name, *Bandstand*, in the earlier years). Dick Clark often interviewed the teenagers on the show to see what they thought of the music being played, and usually at least one musical act would perform on the show stage.

I remember one of Janet's favorite television shows was the medical drama, *Marcus Welby, M.D.* The drama aired from 1969-1976 and starred

Robert Young as the older family doctor with a pleasant manner whose methods conflicted with the more strait-laced methods of Dr. Steven Kiley, who was played by the dashing actor, James Brolin, whom Janet was crazy about at the time.

Another favorite show of hers was *The Big Valley,* which was a western centered on the Barkley Ranch, with a widowed mother played by Barbara Stanwyck, who had a beautiful daughter, Audra (played by Linda Evans), and three handsome sons, Jarrod, Nick, and Heath (played by Lee Majors).

One of my favorite shows was *The Virginian* which starred James Drury, known only as The Virginian, and my favorite character, Trampas, played by the handsome young actor, Doug McClure. The show aired in the 1960s through the early 1970s, and was based on The Shiloh Ranch in the Wyoming territory.

Alias Smith and Jones was another favorite of mine which aired in the early 1970s. It was about two notorious outlaws of the old west, Hannibal Heyes and Kid Curry, now Alias Smith and Jones. A territorial governor promised them amnesty since they had never killed anyone; however, he makes an agreement with them that they have to stay out of trouble for a considerable amount of time; until then, they are still wanted.

Gunsmoke was another western, and a family favorite, starring James Arness as Marshall Matt Dillon, Ken Curtis as Festus Haggen, (the deputy who replaced Dennis Weaver from earlier episodes), Milburn Stone as Doc Adams, and Amanda Blake as Miss Kitty Russell, who ran the saloon in Dodge City, Kansas. Marshall Dillon and Miss Kitty never married on the show, but they were a long-time couple; Festus and Doc argued continually, and if you didn't know better, you would have thought they despised each other; yet they were both good-hearted and would have given their right arm for each other if the need arose. Marshall Dillon was a big man, both in stature, and in respect from the people of Dodge City; he kept the peace in town, along with Festus, and the scripts written for the show often portrayed emotional stories with happy, if not ideal endings.

Black Walnut Festival

Mom and Dad gave me an art set and I loved to draw, especially with charcoals. I entered one of my charcoal drawings in the local contest at the Black Walnut Festival one October.

I had a large sketch pad so I drew my picture much larger than the sample drawing in the book. This was more difficult because I couldn't go exactly by the size of the outlines that they used; I had to improvise.

At the festival, I noticed someone else had the same drawing. I suppose they had received the same art set my parents had bought me. However, the other picture was smaller, about the size of the drawing in the book and was in a black frame. It did look very neat. I didn't know to frame mine; I hadn't entered anything before. The other picture won the blue ribbon for first place and I won the red ribbon for second place. I wondered later if mine would have won the first place if I had thought ahead to frame it.

Unlikely Passenger

Grandma Maze often came to visit us after we moved to Walton. Her home was on the Munday road, below Big Bend. One particular visit, she had stopped to pick up a passenger on the way. When she arrived at our house, we could tell she was tickled about something. She told us she wanted us to see who had traveled with her, so we walked out to the car. There in the passenger seat, still secure in the seatbelt, was a German chocolate cake which had been "riding" along with her all the way from Calhoun to Roane County. It was a very nice surprise for us, and it survived the journey quite safely, thanks to Grandma's quick wit.

Making Homemade Ice Cream

Unlike many families who churned ice cream in the summertime, we often made it in the winter. Huge icicles would form across the road from our house (the water or melting snow would run off the hill and freeze) and that gave us plenty of free ice to put in our ice cream maker. Mom cooked the custard until it coated the back of a wooden spoon; let it cool, and then poured it in the silver canister with the white paddles and placed the lid on it. Then Dad crushed the ice and placed it around the outside of the canister and put rock salt on top of the ice.

My brothers and I took turns churning the ice cream – no electric ice cream maker for us back then. When it was ready, Mom removed the plastic paddle. Whoever could grab it the quickest, got to lick it like licking the spoon when making a cake. Then Mom dished out some for each of us. We backed up to the stove to try to keep warm while eating ice cream on a winter day.

Chapter 7
Coming-of-Age

Awakening

I recall many incidents of 1975 that followed my heart's awakening.

Wayne was the object of my affections, and I was happy when he talked to me in study hall that first day after our high school Christmas vacation, January 2, 1975. I was a junior in high school. The following day he stopped in the hall, so I had to run into him. A few days later, he was late for classes but came in at noon. He had gotten up late, had two flat tires and ran out of gas.

A couple days later in our study hall, he told me all about Lisa. At first, I didn't want to accept the fact he liked her. She didn't go to our school, but lived in a neighboring county. The next day, I stayed overnight with Janet. We watched Elvis on the late movie, which took my mind off Wayne, temporarily.

Diary Entries Beginning January 12, 1975 (Age 17): The grammar is atrocious, but who would have thought these diary entries would be read years later by anyone other than myself.

Dear Diary,

Jan. 12 - Grandma Richard and Denzil came down to visit. We got 6 ½ inches of snow this afternoon. It snowed into the night and we didn't have to go to school for two days.

Harold and I were in the same grade at school, and we attended the same church, the little white Nazarene church in Walton. He was tall with light blond wavy hair and blue eyes. Harold had a quirky way about him; very witty, and always seemed to be joking around, yet he found out what things were really important in life.

Jan. 26 - I went to church today. I found out that Harold got saved last week and I think that's great.

Jan. 27 - We got our report cards today. I made three A's and 2 B's. Dwight (Randy's brother) talked to me on the bus today. He asked me what I made on my report cards.

Wayne was tall with light brown hair and a smile that could melt a girl's heart. I always let on like he was pestering me, but I knew it was just his way of getting my attention.

Jan. 28 - Today Wayne pestered me to death in study hall, along with Larry and Joel.

Jan. 29 - I talked to Wayne today in study hall. When we were walking to the bus, I saw him in the gym windows. He saw me and smiled and waved.

If I fell in the creek now on a cold day in January, I probably would be horrified. But when you're young, things like that seemed much more tolerable, and it wasn't as easy to ruffle my feathers.

Jan. 30 - Yesterday, Janet and I waded the creek – in January, of all times! We were trying to stay on the rocks when we were crossing the creek but we fell in so we just decided to wade the rest of the way across.

It's a wonder Janet didn't ring Wayne's neck; he was so mischievous. Boys! I guess we couldn't live with them or without them…

Jan. 31 - Today Janet and Wayne hid each other's books in study hall. He tied her notebook to the string on the window shade and hung it out the window!

Going to church has been an important part of my life ever since Grandma Richard took me with her when I was a little girl. However, I haven't always been as faithful as I should. There's nothing like the peace you feel when everything's right between you and the Lord.

Feb. 2 - I must say this is the happiest day of my life. This morning I went to church and tonight I went and got right with God again… I want to live the kind of life God would have me to live and some way win souls to God.

Feb. 3 - I'm very happy and I have wonderful peace in my heart.

Catching a glimpse of Wayne, especially when he was being sweet, was the highlight of my day.

Feb. 4 - Wayne was in the gym windows as we went home from school today. He waved at me.

When you're stuck in the house due to bad weather, it seems like forever from February until spring. We might have an occasional pretty day in February, but most of the time the ground is soft and muddy from the melting snow. I longed for the spring and summer days when we could walk through the meadows and hills and pick wildflowers.

Feb. 6 -I wish summer was here. I'm tired of this awful weather.

Feb. 7- Thank goodness today is Friday. I'm tired of school. Today is Linda's birthday.

Feb. 9 - I went to church this morning and tonight.

It would be nice for my best friend to get a telephone; but as we just lived a stone's throw away, we saw each other nearly every day anyway. Of course, it would be nice when the boys started calling her.

Feb. 10 - Janet is supposed to get her telephone today.

Feb. 11 - Tonight Janet and I went to a basketball game. We lost to Spencer 58 – 70.

There was an Art Display at Walton High by a local artist. The article in the Spencer newspaper read as follows: "Phillip Arabia, owner of Arabia's

Art Gallery near Speed [a few miles outside of Spencer], was at Walton High School on Thursday, February 12, and presented an art display of many of his fine works. While there, Arabia answered many of the student's questions and painted a picture for the students to view...."

It was exciting to have a real artist visit our school, and one that lived in our local area. I know Wayne was just teasing me when he asked me who I was taking to the Prom. Oh, how I wish he would have asked me!

Feb. 12 -Today, Wayne and Robbie drove me crazy in study hall. Wayne asked me who I was taking to the prom!

Valentine's Day passed without anything earth-shattering happening – again. I loved the Valentines parties we had when we were in grade school; all the hot dogs and brownies we could eat, fixing up valentines with the little white envelopes for all our classmates. Those days were so innocent and carefree.

Feb. 14 - Today is Valentine's Day.

Janet got a long pink dress for the Prom. I wondered what kind of dress I would get. I pictured a long, flowing dress with sheer sleeves...just as Anne in *Anne of Green Gables* longed for a dress with "puffed" sleeves, which her beloved Matthew bought for her.

Feb. 15 - Today is Saturday. I didn't see Janet today. She went to Spencer. She got a real pretty pink dress – a long one!

Berneice could be such a pain; she liked to stir up trouble. She must have stayed up nights trying to think of ways to aggravate me!

Feb. 16 -Today is Sunday. I went to Sunday school this morning. Harold wasn't there... Tonight Harold was there. He said for me to sit with him. I did. Then Berneice came and sat between us!

Mom usually baked homemade German chocolate cakes for our birthdays as that was our favorite. Since Jay and Alan's birthdays are only one day apart, she would usually bake Jay a full-size cake and bake Alan a little one to match. This way they could blow out their candles together.

Feb. 17 - Today was school! (Ugh) Today was also Jay's birthday. He is 15.

Feb. 18 -Today is Alan and Mary L's birthdays. Alan is 5 and Mary is 17.

The shag haircut was "in," and I wanted mine cut that way, too. Looking back over our yearbooks, it seemed to be the haircut of many of our classmates.

Feb. 19 -Today Janet went to the beauty parlor and got her hair cut in a shag. It looks really cute...

Being in the National Honor Society was a big deal to me. I wish Wayne could have been at the banquet to share this special time.

Feb. 20 -Today I became a member of the National Honor Society. Wayne did, too. And tonight we had a banquet. Wayne didn't go, but I did. Too bad! Today in study hall I said bye to Wayne before I went to the typing room... He said, "Where are you going?" I said, "To the typing room." He said, "Can I go?" It liked to have shocked me to death.

Feb. 21 - Today I asked Wayne why he didn't go to the banquet. He said he had to help his father work.

Finally, a nice day in February. Freedom! We were able to go walking today. I was so glad to be outside and share the day with Janet.

Feb. 22 -Today was Janet's birthday. She is 17. It was a warm day. Janet and I went for a walk up the creek and up McKown's Creek.

Feb. 23 -Today we went up to grandma's. I went to church tonight. Harold wasn't there.

Feb. 25 -Janet got her phone in today.

Feb. 26 -Tonight I went to prayer meeting. Harold was there.

Mr. Richardson was one of my very favorite teachers, and I thought he was so handsome. How silly girls can act over an innocent note.

Feb. 27 -Today I called Mr. Richardson "dear." I didn't mean to. Thank heaven he didn't hear me.

Feb. 28 -Today 5th period Kathi wrote a note and said she was going to tell Mr. Richardson that I called him "dear." I wrote back and told her not to tell him I said he was handsome. He got hold of that note and I almost died.

I hated oral book reports. I'd much rather have written it out. I was so nervous about giving an oral book report in front of the class that I would be sick for days in advance. As much as I've always loved books, you wouldn't think it would be so hard.

March 1 -I finished my book report today finally. I went to church tonight. Harold was there. He sat beside Berneice.

March 2 -Today I went to Sunday school. Tonight I went to church. Harold wasn't there. But Linda told Scotty that I liked Harold. I said I didn't, and he said I needed to go to the altar and get forgiven for lying. Linda about died laughing.

The boys fished for information, trying to find out which girls liked them. Kootsie was Berneice's sister; she was blond, unlike Berneice, and she had the most mischievous grin! She always looked like she was up to something.

March 3 -Today I told Harold not to listen to Scotty if he talked to him.

March 4 -Today Scotty told Harold I liked him.

March 10 -Harold likes Berneice and Berneice likes Wayne. What a mess!

March 12 -I went to church tonight. Harold sat with Kootsie.

March 14 -...Harold told me today that he was going to move to Florida for 3 or 4 months. I'll miss him.

Writing notes in church was probably not the preacher's idea of paying attention, if he had known, but I suppose it's much better to write notes in church than to get into mischief, or worse, somewhere else.

March 15 -I went to Revival tonight. Linda and Berneice weren't there. Harold sat with me. Kootsie sat on the other side of me. They wrote notes to each other. I think they tried to make me jealous. Kootsie got saved tonight...

March 16 -I went to Sunday school and church tonight. There was a missionary there tonight. He talked and showed slides. Some of them were of his son, Scott. He's a doll.

We may have lived in a small community, but books and pictures of foreign places opened up a whole new world to us. Mr. Richardson tried to expand our vision far beyond our little community of Walton, West Virginia.

March 17 -Mr. Richardson showed us slides of his brother when he was in Europe. His brother Larry is a doll.

March 18 -We saw slides again in World Culture and Geography.

March 19 -Tomorrow's the first day of spring.

What I'd been waiting for was finally here – Spring!

March 20 -Today was a beautiful warm day. Janet and I walked to the store. Then we took a walk up McKown's Creek. We went by Randy's house…

Under the bridge, at the mouth of McKown's Creek, was a dependable fishing spot until one day when Janet and I went fishing there and Janet hooked a big turtle on her line. There were some men working at a pumping jack just a few yards away, checking the amount of oil in the big tank nearby, so we didn't dare pull the turtle out of the water while they were there. We just pretended like we weren't getting any bites. We didn't want them to know what a predicament we were in, or that we didn't have the faintest idea how to get the turtle off the line. Another time when we were at McKown's Creek, we were watching the scenery…

March 21 - Today was even a prettier day than yesterday. Janet and I took a walk up the creek. We went up in the woods above the bridge at McKown's Creek to watch those men get the rocks for the bridge in Walton. There was a guy down below us that we didn't see for a while. We were talking and we didn't know he was even there. He heard us after a while and saw us. He talked to us, too. He said we should come down so he could see us better. He asked us what our names were. I told him. Janet didn't talk much. He sure was cute.

Randy was a boy that lived up McKown's Creek, a few miles from our house. He was already out of school. He had a motorcycle and he rode up and down the road. He seemed a little bit on the wild side, different from the boys in school. Maybe that's why he interested me…

March 22 -It rained about all day today. Me and Mom met Grandma Maze at town today to shop. I had fun. This evening when I was waiting on my ride to church, Randy and his dad went up. I guess Randy told his dad to blow the horn because his dad doesn't know me. Randy waved, too.

Oh, what games we play…

March 24 -…Harold was absent today. Mary and Linda said Harold told them that he just says he likes Berneice to make me jealous. Mary said he told her that he didn't like Berneice! (P.S.) Wayne came back to school today.

Construction was going on in Walton. They were building a new bridge across the Poca River, and some of the guys that were doing the construction were good looking. I guess I caught their eyes too…

March 25 -…Today one of those guys that drives those big trucks that haul rocks for the bridge in Walton blew the horn and waved at me every time he went by.

Wayne was such a tease. He knew that I like him; I guess that's why he picked on me so.

March 26 -Today was interesting! In study hall today Wayne and I were talking and I was teasing him about taking Berneice out. He said, "Why don't you go out with me?" I said, "Lisa would get mad." He said, "If that's all you're worried about, I'll take care of that." I was sure surprised.

Danny was a boy Mary was interested in. He didn't go to our school. She saw him while visiting friends who lived in Speed, a few miles out of Spencer. I never met him, but I think he must have been a real heartbreaker.

March 27 -Mary said today is Danny's birthday.

March 30 -Today is Easter. I went to church today and tonight.

When I was growing up, I was always falling and skinning my knees. I either ran and fell, or fell off my bicycle and skidded in the gravels. I probably had more scars from that than anything else.

April 4 -I went to a wiener roast tonight at the 4-H Grounds. I fell and skinned my knee.

If I'd been doing more "studying" in study hall, maybe I wouldn't have gotten a "C" on my report card. I usually got As and a few Bs sometimes, but Cs were out of the question. Perhaps the subjects that interested me weren't in my books...

April 7 - The beginning of another school week... Ugh. I got my report cards – 3 As, 1 B, and a C.

Of course Wayne was taking Lisa to the prom. I don't know why he wanted to torment me so.

April 8 - Today, Wayne asked me if he could have the first dance at the prom. I guess he was joking.

Peggy was a pretty blond-haired girl in my class who was a friend of mine. She had her own car. It was red and white; I think it might have been a Chevelle or something like that. She drove it to school, and I remember hearing her jingling her keys before class started. That was a little unusual back then, since not too many students had their own cars.

April 9 - Today was Peggy and Mr. Richardson's birthdays.

We loved the prom. However, my hairdo was another story, entirely. I had gone to Spencer to a beauty shop to have my hair "put up" as this was a special occasion. But the woman that fixed my hair teased and teased it; then she wound it around in big coils and pinned it all over my head. I looked like I had a big beehive on top of my head. I had to use Mom's fabric softener the next day just to get a brush through it.

April 11 - Tonight was the prom. Me and Janet both had a ball. Us girls danced to fast dances a lot. Greg asked me to dance once. I did. Janet danced with Dexter and Kevin.

The construction workers kept my days interesting…

April 14 - Today that guy that drives one of those trucks went up. Every time he saw me, he waved. Once, he threw me a kiss.

April 15 - Peggy and the girls at school want me to be the princess at the school carnival. They want Wayne to be the prince. But I know he won't do it.

April 18 - Today is Friday. Me and Wayne and Janet went to the typing room. Wayne and me fight all the time.

April 19 - Today was an exciting day. Janet and I walked to the store. And then this evening, we walked up McKown's Creek. Randy was riding his motorcycle. He had a wreck. On the way back from our walk, we saw him.

Wouldn't it have been something if Wayne and I were voted prince and princess of the school carnival? Alas, it was not to be.

April 21 - Another school day. Ugh! We voted for princess of the carnival today. Cheryl and me were the only ones nominated. I lost by 2 or 3 votes.

April 22 - Janet and Me went for a walk up the creek. We went to the mouth of McKown's Creek, but we didn't walk up the road…

I missed Wayne, but found other things to keep me occupied…

April 23 - Today and yesterday I talked to Benny in study hall. He's nice. Wayne has been absent all week so far.

April 24 - Wayne came back to school today. He has had the strep throat since Saturday.

Weren't we the modest ones? Back then, underwear was really meant to be worn under your other clothes, unlike some you might see today.

April 25 - I about died in study hall of embarrassment. Harold got hold of my arm and was pulling it. He had a hold of my sweater and pulled it off my shoulder! Wayne and the whole room saw my bra strap. They all about cracked up laughing.

Then Harold took my purse and didn't give it back. I don't have any idea where it is.

In the 1970s, paneling your walls was the style.

April 26 - I got my room paneled today. We still have the ceiling and window and door facings to do yet.

April 27 - I went to church this morning and tonight. Janet and I walked up to Mynes' today, then up the creek.

April 30 - I saw Randy today. He rode on his motorcycle and stopped beside the bus house over at the road, then turned around and went back up the road.

Fleshman's farm was up McKown's Creek. We loved to explore different roads and hills, and we found a sweet-smelling bouquet for our efforts.

May 2 - This evening Janet and me went for a walk up towards Fleshman's but we took another road. We walked a long way. We found a lilac bush and picked us a bouquet…

May 3 - Janet and I walked to the store today. Janet and Mrs. Walker are supposed to go to Timmy and Martha's shower tonight.

My Junior Class picture in the *Waltonian* was awful. If straight hair would have won a prize, I should have gotten it.

May 6 - I got my yearbook today…

Kathi was a friend of ours. She had short, wavy brown hair, and wore glasses. She was so cute when she got tickled about something; she would put her hand over her mouth and giggle.

May 9 - Tonight Janet and I went to the carnival. Janet worked after a while and me and Kathi walked around a lot.

My bedroom looked like a typical girl's room – all pink and white trimmed. Three walls had brown paneling, but Mom and I put wallpaper on the fourth wall, to brighten up the room. My wallpaper was white with a delicate pink print in it; my bedspread was white with pink flowers and my curtains on the windows were white lace, as was the curtain hanging over my closet (as I didn't have a closet door). I had a round table beside my bed with a white tablecloth and a pink topper; my pink and white lampshade had a ruffled design. There was a darker pink throw rug beside my bed which kept me from stepping out on the cold, hardwood floor in the mornings.

May 10 – Janet and me walked to the store today. My room is all finished now.

May 11 - Today is Mother's Day and Tammy's birthday. I went to Tammy's 3rd party today. We had a blast.

May 20 - Today was the last day for the seniors. They have tomorrow as sneak day.

We went up to Wirt and Calhoun counties to visit our Grandmas and other family who came in to visit during the Memorial Day weekend. We usually had a picnic together. Later, we would go to both family cemeteries and place flowers on the graves of our relatives.

May 25 - Today we went up to both grandmas and both cemeteries although tomorrow is supposed to be the new Memorial Day.

Those crazy boys in study hall; they acted like Veterinarians!

May 29 - Today Mr. Dudding wouldn't take us outside and we had to sit in study hall all day. Benny sat in front of me and Ricky sat behind me. I don't know how they got talking about horses, but they started teasing me. Ricky got a hold of my foot and said he was going to check my hooves. Then he started to open my mouth to see how old I was. Benny said I was about 12. Then Benny said I was going to have a colt in June.

Field Day was held at the 4-H Grounds at Gandeeville, a few miles from Walton. We played games and had a lot of fun.

May 30 - Today was field day. We had a blast, but Janet and me got a bad sunburn.

June 1 - I couldn't go to church this morning or tonight because my sunburn hurts even worse. I sure hope it feels better in the morning.

June 5- Ricky got mad at me today. I think it was because I was with David yesterday. He was still mad today but he said he wasn't. Cindy was on the field today so David was with her...

June 6 - Today was the last day of school. I guess I'm glad we are out of school because I didn't like class (except sixth period) but I miss my friends already. Seems like I've got so many more friends this year (boys mostly). Like David, Wayne, Ricky, Benny and a lot of others. I'll be a senior when school starts! I can hardly wait.

Berneice could be so conniving, and she had a knack for getting things her way.

June 7 -Tonight Roger [Miller] took me, Berneice, Kootsie and Harold to the Youth Crusade at Spencer High School. It was a great service. I think 80-some people got saved. There was a guy there named Terry that is a Christian. Man, would I like to get to know him better. I think he's about the cutest guy I ever saw...we went to the Dairy Queen afterward. We played the jukebox and waited for someone to take our order, but we finally decided to go to the Queen Bee. But it was closed and we ended up going to the Pizza Shack. It was open. We had to take Harold home. He lives way up Harmony. After that, Berneice said, "Roger, why don't you let Debbie ride out the ridge with us?" He said he didn't care. When we got to my house he asked me if I wanted him to stop. I said, "I guess" but I don't think he even heard me because Berneice yelled, "No! She's going to ride on out with me." I rode all the way back with him alone. Berneice thought it was funny.

Jones Park was just below Grandma Maze's, about a half mile away. It wasn't like a big state park or anything like that. It was like being in the country with trees and the river for company.

June 14 - Today we went camping up at Jones Park in Calhoun County. There were lots of people there but we found a camping area to ourselves out away from anyone else. It was a beautiful place under the tall trees and by the riverbank...

Dad was going to seine bait and he wanted me to carry the minnow bucket. Our seine was a large net with sinkers on one edge and floats on the other. We would let it down in the water, and then we would hold the ends together, pulling it up out of the water, catching minnows for bait. We had a silver minnow bucket which had holes in it for air, but the lid rotated so we could open and close it without losing the minnows.

June 15 -This morning was pretty and sunny. Dad said if I carried the bucket while he seined bait, that he might stop in Spencer on the way home and look at that bike that I wanted. I almost fell over. Aunt Betty, Grandma Maze and Marsha came down to visit with us today. Marsha talked to me a good bit. They left and Grandma Richard and Denzil came down for supper. We were just about done eating when it started raining. I went home with them. I didn't think I could stand it another day without taking a bath and washing my hair.

June 16 -This morning Mom, Dad, and Jay came over to Grandma's about ten o'clock. I'd only been up about an hour when they came.

On June 17, we finished camping. Dad bought my bike for me on the way home. My brother Joe came in on leave from the Navy.

June 17 -Today was our last day...

(P.S.) I got my bike today. Joe came in today.

We went swimming in Elk River on Route 4, between Clendenin and Clay. I thought I was doing pretty good teaching myself to swim until Mom yelled at me and told me to come closer to the shore. I just stopped when she yelled at me instead of continuing to tread water. She came in after me, and I was so terrified that I pulled her under with me; Dad had to come in and rescue both of us.

June 27 -Today we all went swimming up Elk River. I learned how to swim a little bit. It was fun till I got in over my head and Dad and Mom got me out.

It was nice having my big brother home, especially when he would take us places. Sometimes, he drove too fast, though. But, if I complained, I knew he wouldn't take me with him. Once in cold weather, he slammed on the breaks, yelled really loud, and rolled his window down to let the cold air in. He called it playing "Freeze Out" and he said that if I complained, well…I just didn't get to go any place with him anymore. So, as crazy as it sounds, I went along with him.

June 28 -Tonight Joe took Janet and me to the movies at Clendenin. We saw The 7th Voyage of Sinbad and True Grit.

June 29 -This morning in Sunday school class, Harold told us that Wayne got saved. I was really glad.

June 30 - Today, Joe took me and Janet up to Grandma's. We didn't stay too awful long, but we had a nice visit.

July 4 - Today we went to Grandma's for the 4th of July. We took a picnic lunch and ate at Grandma Richard's house. We visited a while then went over to Grandma Maze's. Uncle Roger, Aunt Helen and Anthony were there. So was Aunt Betty's family, except Gail and Linda.

We went to the Robey Theater on Main Street in Spencer, which was a vaudeville house before it began showing silent films in the early 1900s, and it may have been the first moving picture show for many locals. It was remarkable that the historic theater was still operating more than a hundred years later.

July 5 - This evening, Joe took me and Jay and Janet to the movies in Spencer. We saw Young Frankenstein. There was a guy who sat behind me that was cute; when I got up to buy a coke, he got up and went back there, too. I knew he was watching me. He came back to his seat a little after me…when the movie was over and we were leaving, he got a hold of my hand. When we got outside, I started walking fast. Joe and Jay were already ahead of us. He asked me where I was running off. I just went ahead.

Kathy and Roger lived out Ambler Ridge. Roger and Dad both worked for Pennzoil in the oil fields. Kathy and Mom were friends and enjoyed sharing recipes.

Aug. 1 -Today we went out to Kathy & Roger's. They are redecorating one of their rooms. Dad, Mom, and Jay helped.

Aug. 2 -Today Mom, Dad, and Jay went out to Kathy's again. They finished the room.

It was time to get ready to go back to school – how the summer flies.

Aug. 6 -We went to Charleston today. I got me some school clothes.

Kay and Larry Cottrell lived up Johnson's Creek, which was a few miles out of Walton, going toward Spencer. I stayed with her two boys one day and had a good time.

Aug. 8 -Today, I babysat for Kay C. I went to her house and watched her two little boys, Ricky and Jeff. I got my cat today. I named him Muffin.

Someone new caught my attention for a few weeks in the late summer of 1975 and into the first few weeks of September. His name was Billy.

Aug. 10 -Today I went to Sunday school. Betty brought those two boys that she was talking about bringing to Sunday school. I knew Ernie since he goes up to the high school, but the other guy I didn't know. His name is Billy…He is cute. He wrote me a note and told me I looked good in the dress I was wearing…He asked me if I had a boyfriend. I told Ernie to tell him "no." Betty told me that he was stuck on me.

Aug. 17 -Today I went to Sunday school. Billy was there. I sat beside of him in class. Then he sat with me in church. He gave me his necklace with his name on it. He put his arm around me when he sat with me. I went home with Carolyn today and I sat with Billy in Betty's car. He said they wouldn't let him go to school here because he lives so far up Vicars Ridge or something like that. I hope he can stay here and go to school though. (P.S.) 10:00 p.m. – Billy just called me. He wants a picture of me. He didn't talk very long but he said he would see me Sunday.

Billy called and wanted me to come to the Homecoming, but I wasn't going to be able to because I didn't have a way to get there. He called me several times when I was over at Janet's, and Mom finally hollered for me, so I came home and called him back.

Aug. 21 - …He asked me if I liked him and I told him "yes." Then he asked me if I would go with him and I said "I guess so…"
Aug. 22 - …He said his dad wouldn't let him go to school here…but his mom is going to ask his dad for him…

Mary and her sister, Sandy, lived up McKown's Creek, and Peggy and her family live a little further up the dirt road from them.

Aug. 23 -Me and Janet rode our bikes up to Mary's this evening. Then we walked with Mary and Sandy up to Peggy's. It was dark before we got home.
Aug. 24 -Carolyn came home with me today. Billy didn't get to come to Sunday school today since Betty can't drive. It won't be long before she is supposed to have her baby. Denzil came down today but Grandma was at the Wilson reunion. He took Jay back with him for a week.

Aug. 25 -Cathy called me this morning. She said there is going to be a hill climb down at her house September 28, which is on a Sunday, and she wants me to come home with her after Sunday school so I can see it. Billy is going to do it. Cathy said he could do it easy but Ernie couldn't. I told Mom and Dad but they haven't answered me yet. I don't think they want me to go. It has been three days since Billy called me!

Billy called me several times the last few days of August. He got approved to attend school at Walton. There was a church picnic that I went to, but he wasn't there. He did call me when I got home and told me he would be at church the next morning.

Aug. 31 -Billy came this morning. Of course he sat with me. Roger preached his farewell message this morning. He said something about some of us loving each other. Billy looked at me and said, "Yeah, I sure do." I about died. I didn't think he would say that – yet, anyway. He held my hand and put his arm around me. I will see him Tuesday.

The first day of school of my senior year and I got in trouble – quite out of character for me. I always liked Mr. Kerby. I didn't get off on the right foot with this new teacher at all. I guess she thought I was being a smart aleck, but I wasn't.

Sept. 2 -Today was the first day of school. Ugh! Would you believe I got yelled at already? Mr. Kerby resigned and some young girl took his place. I can't stand her. I only caught a glimpse of Billy a couple times. He didn't see me though. Billy called me tonight. Guess what! He's a sophomore! I thought he was a freshman but he just has to take 9th grade English over. He's taking Driver's Ed. so I guess he'll get his license pretty soon after all. He asked me what my middle name was. I told him Elaine. He said it. It sounded pretty the way he said it. I'll get to see him tomorrow.

The first two weeks of the new school year Billy was very attentive to me. I saw him at noon, and we would often sit under a shade tree on the school grounds. When the bell rang and we were going back in to class, he would sometimes kiss me. One day at noon, he gave me a little ring with a heart on it.

Sept. 14 -It was a little after nine and Billy hadn't called so I called him. We talked until 11:00. He told me he loved me very much.

I never knew College Day could be so exciting. Ralph was the main attraction for me. How quickly our affections can change. Ralph worked at the Big Star grocery store in Spencer where Mom did most of her shopping.

Sept. 19 -We had College Day at Spencer High School. It was for Walton seniors and Spencer seniors. Guess who I saw, Ralph!! Ralph is a senior too. He works in the Big Star. He saw me today. He said, "Hi, Debbie." He watched me about all the time I was over there. When we were leaving, he came over to me and asked me where I lived. He knew I lived at Walton but not just where I lived. I told him about a mile on the other side of Walton. I didn't have time to talk to him anymore because we had to leave. Once, when me and Kathi and some of the rest of us were sitting on the table in the cafeteria, he had some boy to come over and tell me he wanted to talk to me. I didn't go over where he was. That was later when he came over and asked me where I lived.

Oct. 9 -Today we got off from school. We went to Spencer. We went to the Big Star. Ralph was working! When we went in, Ralph saw me. He said, "Hi, Deb." When he came back in, he kept his eyes on me all the time I was in there (when I was in sight, that is). Of course, I kept looking at him too. He had a longing look (I guess you would say) in his eyes. When we checked out, he was our carryout. He said, "Bye, Debbie."

It was so exciting for Janet and me to catch the Greyhound bus and go to the Black Walnut Festival all by ourselves. How grownup we felt.

Oct. 11 -Today was the Black Walnut Festival. Janet and I caught the bus to Spencer. We had a lot of fun at the carnival (although some of the rides made us sick). I saw Billy at the carnival. We talked a while. He was very friendly to me but it was just like friends. I saw his mother. At noon, Janet and I walked down the bypass. We saw Janet's mom and dad. Her dad gave Janet the key to the car so we could leave our jackets in it. We walked a good ways to the car. On the way back, I saw Ralph. He was sitting on the sidewalk with Larry and that cute blond guy that works with them in the Big Star. I punched Ralph because I saw him first. He said, "Hi, Debbie. What do you say?" Larry said, "Hi, Debbie," and that blond guy said "Hi, Debbie" too. I never even spoke to him before. I talked Janet into going back where they were. I said, "Can we sit down here?" One of them – Larry or the blond – said "no." He was teasing. He said, "As long as Ralph's woman doesn't see you." Well we sat down anyway. I asked Ralph if he wanted me to leave. He said, "No, I don't care." About then, his girlfriend came walking down the other side of the street. One of the boys said, "Oh no, Ralph, this is the end of your love life." He yelled at her and she came over and sat on the other side of him. She didn't say a word to me. She said, "Where have you been, Ralph? I've been looking all over for you." He talked to me more than he did her. He kept saying little things to me about the parade. Once he said, "Why aren't you out there, Debbie?" He sat close to me. I was leaning right against him. I mean he was sitting there. I wasn't trying to touch him, like being flirting. I don't think she liked me at all. (No love lost!!) When the parade was over (or about over) she said, "Ralph, when do you have to go back to work?" He said, "As soon as this is over." He yelled at all the girls in the parade and everything. She was awful quiet. I didn't know if she got mad, but I think she did. (ha! ha!). When we got up to leave (he never even held her hand while we was sitting there) he just said, "See you later." He never even touched her. As soon as he told her "see you later," he said, "Bye, Debbie" right in front of her. I know she didn't like that! It like to have tickled me to death! We, Janet and I, went back up to the carnival then and rode a couple of rides. Then we went to buy our tickets. The bus came and stopped in front of the cafeteria. We were getting ready to get on the bus when a real cute guy came and asked the bus driver if he would wait for him. I was kidding Janet. I said, "He can sit with me." When he got on the bus, he said "Hi" and sat down beside of me – across the aisle, that is. He was really cute. He was tall and blond with blue eyes. He started talking to me. He introduced himself. He said, "Jay" and reached for my hand. I shook his hand and said, "Debbie Richard." He asked me who my friend was. I told him "Janet." He asked me all kinds of questions like where I was from, the school I went to, did I like school, what classes did I take, and my age and I don't know what all. He told me about him. He said his last name was Nutter. He is 21 years old and lives in Charleston now. He used to live in Spencer and graduated from Spencer High School. He took French when he was a senior. He goes to some kind of school down there. He said he'd like to come back to Spencer. (Boy, I wish he would). He told me he liked my bracelet and my ring. He said, "They look good on you." He smiled a lot. Boy, he was good looking. I'll probably never see him again, although I wish I could.

Oct. 12 -Today is Sunday. Helen called me today. She said she saw Cheryl and Larry yesterday. She said Cheryl and Larry were supposed to bring Ralph by my house so he could know where I lived and ask me out. I don't know if they did or not. I hope so!

My eighteenth birthday came and I've never been out on a real date. Oh, sure I've had my share of admirers and even one or two "going steady" types at school or church, but that's about it.

Dec. 14 -Today is my 18th birthday. It seems hard to believe.

I'm sure glad Ralph wasn't hurt in the wreck (or Harold). I never went out with Ralph. I wish I hadn't been so shy. I mostly saw him when we were grocery shopping.

Dec. 18 -Today Harold came in English class and said, "Me and your old boyfriend had a wreck last night." I said, "Who?" He said "Ralph." Linda said, "That's not her <u>old</u> boyfriend. It's hers now." I found out later that Mary told him I knew Ralph. I guess Ralph never talked to Harold about me. (P.S.) Neither one was hurt.

Dec. 19 -This evening, we went to Spencer to pick up the Bronco. Dad and Jay rode home in the Bronco. Mom and me took the car and went to the Big Star to get groceries. I saw Ralph. He said "Hi" to me. He was our carryout. Mrs. Kinnard was parked beside of us. Mom talked to her a while. Ralph put our groceries in the car. I said, "I heard you had a crash the other night." He said, "Yeah, a small one," and we both glanced at the car. I said, "Yes, I saw your car." One whole side was smashed in. He said "Bye" to me. (P.S.) That's the first time I've seen him since Oct. 11 at the Black Walnut Festival.

Jimmy was in my class. He was such a sweet boy, but his heart belonged to Paula.

Dec. 21 -Tonight we had our Christmas program at church. It was pretty good. I think about Jimmy a lot. He always went down the stairs by Mrs. Mitchell's class after English, but then he started going down the main stairs while I went around to Spanish class. And I go down those stairs to my locker instead of going straight to Spanish. He went down the other side of the stairs than the ones I went down; and now he goes down the stairs right behind me. And when we go to 1st period, he's right behind me sometimes. I about died the other day; I looked around to see if he was coming up the stairs and he was hardly two inches behind me. I caught him looking at me the other day. Linda says he looks over this way a lot in English class. (P.S.) I like Ralph, too.

Grandma Richard and Uncle Denzil came down to Walton to be with us for Christmas that year. We were always together for Christmas, and now some thirty-odd years later, Dad and Grandma are gone, Uncle Denzil is older and unable to travel, and it seems like eons since we were all together, opening presents, laughing, and talking around the family Christmas tree.

Dec. 24 -We opened our presents this evening. I got a watch, a new dress, perfume, and a lot of other stuff.

Dec. 25 - Today is Christmas. Grandma and Denzil came down today. We had a nice time.

Senior Year 1975/1976

Our senior year seemed even more special to me because it was the Bicentennial year, and even our yearbook cover was red, white and blue. Our school colors were green and white, but our class colors were red, white and blue; our class flower was the red rose, our class motto was "Not As We Were, But As We Will Be."

Mark Swiger was president of our class; Vicki Ashley, vice-president; Peggy Paxton, secretary, and Tim Nida, treasurer.

The Senior Hall of Fame voted: Janet & Jim – Best Personality (which I would have to agree with as Janet was my very dear friend, and Jim was one of the cutest boys around); Carolyn & Harold – Wittiest (they were both cut-ups and always clowning around); Jim & Peggy – Most Likely to Succeed; Vicki & Jim – Best All Around (Vicki is still working at the bank as far as I know, and Jim is a high school teacher, following his interest in Agriculture and Horticulture, and I'm happy for their success); Teresa & Kenny – Quietest; Cathy & Calvin – Best Dressed; Carolyn & Harold – Loudest; and Pat & Walter – Best Athlete.

My senior activities included Spanish Club, the Bible Club, member of FHA (Future Homemakers of America), and the National Honor Society.

I often helped out the FFA (Future Farmers of America) by typing for them (thanks to my typing teacher, Mr. David Kinison). I think I've kept all of my shorthand and typing papers. We had to do typing drills to make sure our fingers were on the "home" keys – asdf and jkl; and then we graduated to sentences such as "Your mind is like a good knife; it must be used often to remain sharp." Or "We start many jobs that we never finish." And "A full sheet of typing paper is 8 ½ by 11 inches and contains 66 lines." Then we moved on to other typing projects. As I said, this was a typing class with typewriters; this was before computers. We had to learn to count spaces to know where we wanted our margins to be, or to center a typing assignment on the page. We didn't have the luxury of hitting a computer format key to do it for us. We advanced from typing drills and sentences to such assignments as business letters, envelopes, outlines and programs for special events). There was a FFA/FHA banquet my senior year, and I was presented a certificate of appreciation signed by Mr. Cummings, Advisor and Jim Workman, President.

The Walton FFA land judging team excelled that year as reported by the local newspaper May 13, 1976. They came in second in the district competition. Pictured in the newspaper photo were Lois Smith, Jim Workman, Carlos Crihfield, FFA Advisor Paul Cummings, and Harold Ferguson.

Ricky Drake was named Walton High School's "1975-76 Betty Crocker Family Leader of Tomorrow." He won the honor by competing with other seniors in the written knowledge and attitude examination held December 2. His picture, and a considerably large article, was published in the Spencer newspaper. An excerpt reads, "He will receive a certificate from General Mills, sponsor of the annual educational scholarship program, and becomes eligible for state and national honors.... In the spring, state winners and their faculty advisors will be the guests of General Mills on an expense paid educational tour to Washington, D.C. A special event of the tour is the announcement of the All-American Family Leader of Tomorrow, whose scholarship will be increased to $5,000.00."

Our Homecoming Court was well represented by our senior class. Vicki Ashley was our Homecoming Queen, escorted by Ricky Drake; Jim Workman escorted Sherry Burnside, and Mike Botkins escorted Gail Cummings. Our Homecoming and other home football games were held at the 4-H Grounds at Gandeeville, a few miles from Walton. Other events held at the 4-H Grounds were Field Day and the Prom as they had a nice activity building as well.

We had guests at our school one day which had brought new fashions for us to see, and they needed girls to model them in a fashion show for the school. I was picked as one of them, and my outfit was a skirt and striped sweater set. They took our picture modeling in front of the double doors at the entrance of our high school; this picture appears in the front pages of our 1976 yearbook with the caption above it reading, "Ladies who pose with smiles so bright." I'm on the far right in the photo. They also took a picture of us standing in the schoolyard, and I'm the one on the far right in that photo also. This was exciting for a small town school; rarely were we able to participate in anything quite like this.

The Red Cross came to our school to sponsor a blood drive, and Jimmy was among the volunteers recruiting donors. I had never given blood before, and really had no intention of giving this time, but when Jimmy came by and asked me if he could sign me up, how could I refuse? I think he was smiling to himself as he walked away, pleased with himself, no doubt. He probably knew I'd be a "shoe-in" as I was sweet on him at the time.

In my "Memories '76" book, under the heading "Prices Today," are listed: $1.00 for a football or basketball game, .25 would buy a coke, $1.25 would get you into see a movie, a poster cost .75 and a record album cost $6.98. Under "Vacations & Trips," are listed: Anthropology and World Culture Classes got to go to Sunrise [Museum] at Charleston April 29, 1976. Mr. Richardson was our teacher. (The mansion which previously housed the "Sunrise Museum" is also known as the MacCorkle Mansion and is now privately owned and not open to the public. "Sunrise Museum" became "The Avampato Discovery Museum" when it moved into The Clay Center for the Arts and Sciences in Charleston, West Virginia, and opened in 2003. The museum features two floors of interactive science exhibits and an art gallery. Science gallery themes include creativity and engineering; sound, light, and color; ...earth science; health and wellness; and a special area for pre-school age children). Another trip entry in my memories book reads: FHA and Home Ec. Classes went to the Grand Central Mall at Parkersburg on September 24th to see a Sew Fair."

On the autographs pages, are several that I treasure; here are just a few: Janet wrote, "...To a real sweet girl who is as close as a sister..." and from Mary, "...a real sweet girl with a smile for everyone..." Linda wrote, "...You're really a good friend..." My typing teacher, Mr. Kinison, wrote, "...You'll make a <u>good</u> anything you go at..." and Mr. Richardson wrote, "...To a really sweet <u>Lady</u>...."

On Graduation

High school graduation night came. Our foursome – Mary, Linda, Janet and I – posed for a picture on the front steps of our high school, along with our witty classmate, Harold. Each of us were wearing white dresses since our graduation gowns (that we would put on later) were also white, and we were each holding a long-stem, red rose – except Linda because Harold snatched hers and was posing with it. Oh, and by the way, Harold wasn't wearing a white dress.

During the ceremony, we wore the white robes and caps with the tassel on the side. The tassel on my cap, and the satin stole around my shoulders, was gold because I was an honor student. It was a very proud moment for our parents and us.

Cathy Walker gave the Valedictory Address, Ricky Drake gave the Salutatory Address, and Janet, Peggy, and Marie were honor speakers during the ceremony.

After the ceremony, some of the graduates were going to Spencer to eat out and celebrate. Kevin asked me to go with them.

I had never been out on a real date before, so I asked Mom and Dad if it would be ok. They agreed, hesitantly I think.

We had a good time. Afterward, we split up in different cars. Kevin and I went for a drive, and probably talked more that night than we had when we were in classes together. I don't know what cologne he was wearing, but I remember he smelled really nice.

Shortly after graduation, he joined the military, and I went with his family to the airport to see him off and wish him well.

While we were at the airport in Charleston, a man approached Kathy, Kevin's sister. He asked her if she had ever done any modeling. He thought she would make a good model. I'm sure she must have been flattered to have received such a compliment.

The Wreck

After high school graduation, Janet and I planned a trip to Virginia Beach. We had never seen the ocean, and we were so excited to go. We packed our shorts and bathing suits and even a couple of nice outfits for nights on the town. Dad mapped out the route for us. After we packed everything in my two-tone, green Dodge Dart, which had been handed down to me by Dad, we headed out for the sandy beaches and blue waters of the Atlantic.

I still have the note Dad wrote me just before we left for our trip.

"Dear Deborah, I probably won't see you before you go to Virginia Beach, so have a good time but be careful. Don't go in very deep water as you can't swim. You are one of my most prized possessions. Love, Dad."

We traveled through the winding roads and interstates and finally arrived in Virginia Beach. We found a place to park the car, and then we ran down to the beach, kicking our bare feet in the sand until we reached the water's edge, splashing in the water and giggling like carefree children. As far as you could see, there was nothing but water and sky.

We checked into a motel, and had a wonderful time that week, playing in the ocean, combing the beach for seashells, walking along the boardwalk, and exploring the beautiful resort area.

The day we were to start back home, we checked out of the motel and put our luggage and sandy seashells in the trunk of the car, then headed down to the beach for one last dip in the ocean. We pulled our blue jean shorts up over our bathing suits and headed for home with the sting of salt and sand still on our skin.

Nightfall came while we were driving through the mountain roads of West Virginia. There had been a steady rain, and the roads were slick. All of a sudden, I lost control of the car. The steering wheel spun out of control – like something you would see in the movies. The car spun around in the road, and we were heading back the way we had just come, but on the wrong side of the road, towards an oncoming car. Eventually, we sailed across the highway, hit the side of a tree, flew over a rock pile, and landed right side up over the hill (near a river, I found out later, but couldn't see it as it was pitch dark). Later, I realized how much we must have looked like the *Dukes of Hazzard*.

We were so shook up. Janet couldn't get her door opened. It was jammed. I couldn't get my door open either, but I had forgotten to unlock it.

The police and wrecker came… not sure who all else. The wrecker was able to pull our car up in one piece. I remember sitting in a car with a young man while the officer took the report. The young man was the one driving the car that had been behind us, but when our car spun around in the road, he told me that he had pulled over to avoid hitting us. I think he was driving a red Camaro.

I hadn't been through an accident like that before, and hated to call Dad and tell him what happened. I told him that the car was banged up, but I thought we could make it the rest of the way home. I didn't want him to have to come out on a dark, rainy night after us.

As we were driving a short time later, we heard a noise and wondered if something was falling apart on the car. It sounded like something rubbing. I pulled the car over. A trucker stopped and pulled the fender away from my tire, and told me that he thought we could make it the rest of the way if we took it easy, which we did.

We were pretty shaken when we got home, but our parents were both so happy to see us in one piece they weren't too hard on us.

A few days after the accident, I received a surprising phone call from the young man who had witnessed the accident. He told me that he lived in that area, near Rainelle. He hadn't called because he was upset about that night; he called to ask me out on a date. He was very nice, and I was flattered, but I decided not to accept his invitation.

Janet told me later that one corner of the road had been broken away and that caused us to drop off the road, and sent the car spinning out of control. I would never have known what had actually caused it if she hadn't seen that on her side. The road should have been repaired; our wreck could have been fatal. Some think we were very lucky. But looking back now, I realize how very blessed we were.

Chapter 8
Happenings at Home and Abroad

First Telephone Exchange in WV

On May 15, 1880, Wheeling established one of the country's first telephone exchanges. A switchboard setup in the basement of a local bank served 25 subscribers. During the early 1880s, switchboards and lines were installed in Parkersburg, Moundsville, and Clarksburg.

My Aunt Lyla Richard began work for C & P (Chesapeake & Potomac) Telephone Company in Fairmont, West Virginia, around 1950 as a local operator. Subscribers were able to call local residences in the Fairmont area. Aunt Lyla remembered the ringdown system by answering a call, "Number, please?" In telephone language, ringdown is a method of signaling an operator in which telephone ringing current is sent over the line to operate a lamp.

Lyla had left the little community of Munday after high school to seek employment in the city. However, she wasn't entirely among strangers, as she was able to room with her cousin, Jean, while working in Fairmont. Jean was Aunt Thelma's daughter. Aunt Thelma and Lyla's mother, Edna Richard, were sisters. Lyla worked on the local switchboard until the mid-1950s, when she transferred to Clarksburg.

Not only did she find a new position at the phone company when moving to Clarksburg, but also she met Joe Kopshina of Nutter Fort. Nutter Fort is just on the outskirts of the city. Lyla and Joe married, and had a son who they named Jimmy.

At Clarksburg, Lyla started out as a long-distance operator, where she was available to assist with making long distance calls, answering billing questions, making collect calls, and other functions, including emergency assistance. Then, she advanced to a desk job as a service assistant, answering questions and assisting other operators. Next, she became a training instructor, training new operators; this was the job she really loved. Later, the IBM computers came on board, which appeared to be as big as television sets, and quite overwhelming. Learning the computer was new to her, and quite a challenge, but one that she mastered. She retired from the telephone company in 1986 when she was 55 years old. She kept her original headset that she wore while working at the telephone office; it's hanging on her wall at home, beside her antique telephone. The telephone company where Lyla started out in Fairmont is now the Telephone Museum, located on Monroe Street in Fairmont, and is a tribute to telephone history. The museum is available for tours, and contains various switchboards, pay phones, booths, test boards, and cable displays.

The Chesapeake and Potomac Telephone Company of West Virginia began operations on January 1, 1917. C & P of WV took over telephone operations in West Virginia, being served by Southern Bell and C & P Telephone Co. of Maryland. In 1984, The C & P of WV became a holding of Bell Atlantic. The Bell Atlantic was the last Bell Operating Company of Bell Atlantic to provide "party line" telephone service.

I remember having "party lines" at home when I was a child. There could be anywhere from four to six families hooked up on the same party line. I can recall several times being at Grandma Richard's when she picked up her phone to make a call; there would already be someone on the phone, and she'd have to hang up and wait her turn, and try again. Not everyone on the party line was that courteous. Several times when Grandma was on the phone, she would hear somebody on her party line pick up the receiver, and she knew they were listening in on her conversations. It reminds me of how Corabeth Godsey or Miss Fanny at the switchboard listened in on conversations on the television show *The Waltons,* or Mrs. Olsen on *Little House on the Prairie*, listening in to hear, and often spread, local gossip.

1957 Retrospect

A look back at the year 1957 clearly reflects how prices have escalated over the past half century since I was born. The average cost of a new home was $12,220; an average income was $4,494; a Ford car was $1,879 - $3,408; Gas was 24 cents a gallon; and a postage stamp was 3 cents. The average grocery prices were also much lower in 1957: Milk was a dollar a gallon; bread was 19 cents a loaf; bacon was 60 cents per pound; eggs were 28 cents per dozen; Pot roast was 69 cents per pound; and Vermont maple syrup was 33 cents for a 12-ounce bottle.

Notable events included: The movie, *Jailhouse Rock*, starring Elvis Presley, premiered; the book, *The Cat in the Hat* by Dr. Seuss was published; other popular books of that era were *Kids Say the Darndest Things!* by Art Linkletter and *Please Don't Eat the Daisies* by Jean Kerr; Popular music included "Young Love" (Tab Hunter), "Party Doll" (Buddy Knox), "Teddy Bear" (Elvis Presley), "Tammy" (Debbie Reynolds), and "Diana" (Paul Anka). Donny Osmond was born in December of 1957; Elvis purchased a mansion in Memphis which he named Graceland; and the family-oriented television show, *Leave it to Beaver,* premiered on CBS, starring Barbara Billingsley, Hugh Beaumont, Tony Dow, and Jerry Mathers. Other popular TV shows during that time were *Gunsmoke* and *The Danny Thomas Show.*

Harpers Ferry

One year, Mom and Dad, with my younger brother Jay, took a trip to the historic town of Harpers Ferry in Jefferson County, West Virginia. The town was built on steep hillsides where the Potomac and Shenandoah rivers flow together, and where Maryland, Virginia, and West Virginia meet. From the top of the hill, portions of the three states can be seen.

Harpers Ferry is best known for the abolitionist, John Brown, who made his stand against slavery and paid for it with his life. He captured the attention of the nation like no other abolitionist before or since. Some sixteen years later, the Civil War was under way. Harpers Ferry had been a picture-perfect town tucked away in the Blue Ridge Mountains, but was ravaged following the years after John Brown's death.

The National Park Service stepped in and restored many of the buildings of this historic town. Enough of the cobbled streets and original buildings survived, and the restoration project so far has managed to recreate the town without giving it a feeling of a theme park.

Whether they were walking along cobblestoned Shenandoah Street at Lower Town or straight up High Street, Mom remembered there were many things to see, much like the residents did in the mid-19th century. The storekeepers, such as those at Harpers Ferry General Store or The Dry Goods Store, wore period costumes. There were big wooden barrels and wooden wheelbarrows, as well as stacked firewood sitting in front of The Dry Goods Store. The women wore long dresses, often with aprons. A man at Frankel's Men Clothing Store might be seen with a long black coat and trousers, shiny vest, black bowtie, and black hat. St. Peter's Catholic Church towers over Shenandoah Street with its tall steeple. Another landmark Mom remembered is the Harper Ferry Train Station.

The Museum on Shenandoah Street holds decades of history, including guns such as those used during the wars, on display. Looking back, Mom recalled watching a demonstration of how to tap the gunpowder in a rifle, probably much like the one Meriwether Lewis used. It's not unusual to see "Meriwether Lewis" riding his horse down the cobbled streets, or see him climbing the stone steps to The Harper House, the town's only tavern. There was the Provost Marshal Office, where the Marshal acted as judge, jailer and executioner. You might also see the Blacksmith demonstrating his trade, or listen to "Thomas Jefferson" speaking to visitors, dressed in his period attire with black jacket and trousers, a white shirt with ruffles down the front and on the cuffs of his long sleeves. A Farmers Market with a man in a straw hat might be selling watermelons and various kinds of cheeses, with a covered wagon set up nearby. Park Rangers give guided tours and present educational programs for students. Other things of interest to a history buff might be the Cannon at Murphy Farm, the Frontiersmen with their rugged attire, the John Brown Fort, or the Artillery Demonstration.

Mom told me about Jefferson Rock, which is a rock naturally shaped like a table with four legs, and how the view of the surrounding area from up there on the hill was breathtaking.

Other interests for those who may not be history buffs might be rafting on the Shenandoah River, biking, or hiking the trails. Serious hikers might travel across the Potomac River on the pedestrian footbridge — which is actually a railroad bridge — but there is a fence which separates the pedestrian part. As tourists approach the end of the footbridge, they will find that they must walk down a steel spiral staircase. The staircase has an open-grid design through which they can see the woods below.

Scary Movies

It's hard to imagine now that I enjoyed watching scary movies when I was younger, but I did. I used to watch them with Janet at her house, and I imagined every little noise, every creak of a door or window, even the wind blowing, was something out there – something trying to slip up on us. Janet said that I was the world's-worst at imagining things.

One TV movie that was really scary was *I Saw What You Did, And I Know Who You Are!* It was about two mischievous teens who are home alone and begin randomly calling telephone numbers and telling whoever answers, "I saw what you did, and I know who you are!" One call is placed to a man who recently murdered his wife and disposed of her body in the woods. Thinking he's been found out, he comes after the girls. I imagine that if anybody who watched that movie had ever played that prank themselves, they would abandon such a foolish game.

And who could forget *Jaws*, about the gigantic great white shark that terrorized a small island community – and that haunting music just before it strikes?

Stephen King's *Pet Cemetery* was made into a movie, but I was terrified just reading the book. I could watch only a few minutes at the beginning of the movie and had to turn the TV off. I cautioned Janet not to even read the book when she was alone in the house.

A movie that I saw at the movie theater – I think it was at the Robey Theater at Spencer – was *The Amityville Horror*. After that movie, I was afraid to leave the theater, but ran all the way down the alley to the parking lot, and when we pulled up to our driveway, I ran in the house and locked the door. I felt like something was at my heels. That wasn't a movie I soon recovered from. And now, I have no desire to watch anything like it.

Hey, Sailor!

My older brother Joe, who had big dreams of faraway places and sailing on the open seas, was in the Navy for a span of twenty years, of which we saw very little of him. We still have some of his letters he wrote home to us during those first years, and I think learned more about him as a brother, and as a person, through them.

The first one postmarked Nov. 22, 1975, he greeted us "Kumusta Ka." That means "how are you?" (He stated that he is slowly learning the Philipino language). Joe had just left Hong Kong and was able to be at Billy Graham's crusade for two nights while he was there. He was so excited to see him in person.

Jan. 9, 1976 - Writing from the Philippines, he was trying to re-enlist for orders to the Philippines. If he got them, it would be a long time before he made it back to the States, if ever. Nothing would have made him happier than to live in the Philippines. He wanted to buy a house over there in the mountains, but he wanted to do what the Lord wanted him to do.

Feb. 15, 1976 - Joe wrote that he did get his orders to the Philippines for six years. He would be stationed in Subic Bay, Philippine Islands.

Aug. 28, 1976 - Joe wrote to Mom that he hasn't been able to find any Hamburger Helper in the Philippines and admitted without Hamburger Helper his cooking ability was greatly diminished. He asked Mom to send him a bunch of recipes of things he liked – meatloaf, cookies, bread, and other good things. He noted on the back page of the letter that he'd found a house for 100 dollars a month – the Navy gave him 90 dollars a month, so that would only be 10 dollars out of his pocket.

Sept. 22, 1976 - Joe wrote that he decided to stay in the barracks and not live out in town. The houses were just not up to standards and he would need a vehicle if he decided to move out;

Oct. 8, 1976 – Joe wrote to Dad at three o'clock in the morning, telling him that he was going snorkeling with a couple of friends that he worked with, so he should close and get some sleep;

Nov. 13, 1976 - Joe wrote to Dad that he had given it considerable thought, and the best transportation for him over there would be a motorcycle. One of the reasons he gave was, "gasoline is pushing 90 cents a gallon" and "car prices here are about double what they are in the States."

Dec. 3, 1976 - Joe wrote that he finally got a house off base, and that it was really nice for a house over there. He was renting a three-bedroom place with a large living room. He was looking forward to having Bible studies in his new place and having some of his friends on board ship stay with him.

Jan. 27, 1977 - Received letter from Joe; he was on the *USS Enterprise* heading for the Indian Ocean on a 56-day line period with a four-day stopover in Mombasa, Africa. He stated NTCC Subic had a program where you could take short cruises aboard ships, and he took them up on it so he could get in some traveling and see some new ports. Stated he loved to travel and see new places. Getting there was half the fun, too. He loved to go above decks and look out over the water and smell the clean air. At night, there were thousands upon thousands of stars shining in an unpolluted sky, and if you have never seen a sunset at sea, you've never seen a beautiful sunset. He reflected that God sure knew what He was doing when He made this part of the world.

Feb. 28, 1977 - Joe wrote that they are docked off the coast of Mombasa, Africa. He also commented that it was so pretty and peaceful out at sea. One night he took a break and went out on the fantail…it was quiet except for the water and there must have been a billion stars in the sky. That's a setting most people never get to see.

March 21, 1977 – Joe wrote to Dad that at 0800 they would pull back into Subic Bay and he would be a shore sailor again. He said he'd never seen two months fly by so fast, and that he'd enjoyed himself immensely. There was something about the sea that got into his blood. Poets write about the mysteries and the beauty of the sea, and he had found truth in what they say.

May 1, 1977 - Joe wrote that one reason why he was so happy was because he really enjoyed working at the Serviceman's Center and a Christian orphanage. He stated he just recently found out about it, but he went there whenever he could. The children loved to be visited, and he got to push them in the swings, and they just loved to be picked up and hugged. He thought he enjoyed it as much as they did. He felt sorry for them that they didn't have any parents. And he said that he'd like to take this opportunity to thank both Mom and Dad for giving him a good home and a lot of love. That was a blessing that a lot of people don't have, and he was sure glad that he did.

June 21, 1977 – Joe addressed this letter to Mom. He said he was really shocked to hear about Dad. As young as Dad was [43 years old], a heart attack was the farthest thing from his mind. He said he was going to be attending a Bible Conference for the next couple days, and all the people there would be praying for Dad. He asked Mom to please keep him informed how Dad was getting along.

June 29, 1977 – Joe wrote to Mom that he received her letter and he was sure glad to hear that Dad was getting better… he went around telling his friends – the people who had been praying for Dad. Everyone was rejoicing with him…they had prayer and thanked God for His goodness and answer to their prayers;

July 9, 1977 – This letter was addressed to Dad. He told him that Mom had been writing to him, and he was sure glad to hear that he was getting better. He told Dad that when he was feeling up to it, he sure would like to hear from him.

Aug. 4, 1977 – Joe received his orders – NAS Whidbey Island, Washington. "Yahoo!" he exclaimed. One of the guys he worked with was from Washington, and he told him that Whidbey Island was one of the best places in the state. It was great for hunting, fishing, camping, and any outdoor sport. It was close to the Olympic Rain Forests, and everybody on the west coast had heard of how beautiful and majestic that place was.

Dec. 17, 1977 - He wrote, "Dear Folks, I arrived in Whidbey Island yesterday, December 5. It sure is pretty country up here, big pine trees all over the place."

April 26, 1978 – Letter to Dad stated that he supposed we must be wondering why he hasn't written lately. He had been putting off telling us all what happened a little over a month earlier. He was out four wheelin' and he ran off the road and hit a large pine tree. Nobody got hurt, and for that he was thankful. Also, he moved out of the place he was in and moved into a duplex apartment. It reminded him of our old house in Munday, as it had a combined kitchen and dining area, a living room, and two bedrooms.

June 7, 1978 – Joe wrote that he'd been fishing three times in the last two days and hadn't caught one yet. He was going to try a different lake the next time. The only thing he had caught so far was sunburn.

Dec. 2, 1978 – Joe wrote with some good news – as of January16, he'd be an RM2. That's equal to a sergeant in the Army… It meant he'd get forty to fifty dollars more a month and less sweeping and swabbing the decks. Being single, he got stuck with Christmas duty. He would be working sixteen hours Christmas Day.

July 5, 1979 – He wrote that he got called into the front office and was told that he was being transferred to BRAVO section as their supervisor. He was more qualified than some of the others they might have chosen. On a different note, he said that one of their favorite things to do was to drive around and look at the pretty country up there…Going over the mountains in June and July with the tops of them covered with snow was a breathtaking sight.

Sept. 18, 1979 – He wrote that he received his orders…he would be in San Diego for at least three months. He left [Washington] on Dec. 1. The Coral Sea went on a Westpac (Western Pacific) cruise in November. He was not too anxious about going on a cruise early the next year because he would have to make at least one full cruise, and possibly another one, before he got out.

Nov. 2, 1981 – "Hi, Sis…Thought you might like a postcard of Singapore. It's not as pretty as Washington, but it is a nice place to visit…"

Racing

One day when Alan was about six years old, I took him with me to the grocery store in Clendenin. It had snowed and the roads were slick. We were driving along – up and down winding hills – while he told me how fast he was going to drive when he grew up. He made the story sound more and more intense. He was going to drive 120 miles an hour, and on and on the story went. All of a sudden, we hit a slick spot in the road and the car "fish-tailed" a little. Instantly, Alan looked at me very serious and asked, "Deb-wuh" (he couldn't quite say "Deborah" real plain yet), "don't you think you should slow this thing down a little bit?"

I wasn't going very fast but it startled him that we had slid around in the road. This brave little "race driver" quickly changed his mind about going so fast.

"Flooring It"

We lived in a valley between two hills. There was a creek right below our house, and a dirt road ran beside it. We had a bridge that we drove across to get from the main road to our yard. We parked our cars along the edge of the dirt road in the wintertime or in the yard when the weather was nice and the yard wasn't soft and muddy.

In the winter, in order for Mom to make it across the bridge and up the incline to the road, she would back our old green and white Oldsmobile up the hill as far as she could safely go to get a running start, and then she would "floor it," and we went sliding through the snow and ice, across the bridge and up to the main road. We often held our breath, praying we could make it safely to the other side without sliding into the iron pipe rails of the bridge, or landing over the bank and into the freezing water below.

Dad at Dress Up

We used to watch a television show where a chef, Friedman Paul Erhardt, known as "Chef Tell" did cooking demonstrations. He had a jolly personality and German accent, and was known as the "first of the great showman chefs." My dad liked to watch him, and sometimes imitated him in our kitchen. I have a picture of Dad in the kitchen with flour all over his hands and cutout Christmas cookies on the table. He got tickled trying to pretend he was Chef Tell that he could hardly talk for laughing so hard.

Another picture I really like is with Dad standing in the kitchen doorway with a white towel wrapped around his head, and carrying a broom or mop handle. I'm not sure if he was trying to look like a Sheik, as Rudolph Valentino in the movie by the same name, or whether he was trying to look like a shepherd in a Christmas play. But either way, it was certain that he was enjoying himself because he was laughing so hard, and he always cracked us up with his witty imagination.

Chapter 9
A New Beginning

The Heart of the Matter

My younger brother, Jay, is fifty now, but he had his first open-heart surgery when he was only seven years old, and I was nine. We were living at Munday in Wirt County at the time, and the hospital was in Morgantown, West Virginia, more than one hundred miles away. Lula, our very dear neighbor, came and stayed with Joe and me while they were away. I had not been separated from Mom for such a long period of time, and I couldn't understand why I couldn't be with her. Lula tried to explain to me that Jay needed her more right then, but that was hard for a little girl of nine to understand. Lula let me bake cookies with her, and she did all she could to comfort us.

Jay had complications from his first surgery, which hindered him through elementary school and into his teenage years. Although he was very bright, and could remember dates and figures much better than I could, he faced other challenges. Our dad tried for years to get assistance for him through a government plan, but the "red tape" always got in the way. I remember the morning Dad was supposed to go to court; he was very sick with severe chest pains, yet he went anyway as the court date had been set for six months, and he said he couldn't afford to miss the opportunity as it could take months to get another date set. Dad was so strong. I don't know any other man who would put himself through what he did when he was so sick. He went to court, but his attorney didn't speak up on their behalf at all; Dad was so upset when he got back home.

In October 1978 when Jay was eighteen, he had open-heart surgery again. This time the surgery was done at Charleston Memorial Hospital in Charleston, West Virginia. We were living in Walton by this time, and it was the nearest large hospital that performed this kind of surgery. While we were in the waiting room during Jay's surgery, we met a very nice lady named Dot. Her husband, Harv, also had heart surgery. They were originally from England, and I loved to hear Dot talk. She had a lovely accent. We met their daughter and her fiancé. They were married in the hospital so her dad could be at the wedding. Our families became friends, and we kept in touch for some time afterward.

Twenty years later, when Jay was thirty-eight years old, he had to have his aorta valve replaced. This surgery was also done at Charleston Memorial. I was living out of state by then and didn't get to go home to be with him. However, he was married by this time, and his wife, Mary, was with him.

At age forty-four, in January 2005, he had to have a pacemaker put in, and two years later, he had to have it replaced. Jay has had a struggle with his health, to say the least, and has had numerous hospital visits and procedures since then, due to heart disease.

Jay's tough, though. He's had to walk, in various weather conditions, to get to many doctor's appointments or to pick up medicine at the drug store, relying on the goodness of passers-by to give him a ride, at least as far as they were going.

Sometimes, he would ride the little Senior Citizen bus to Spencer ("the old people's bus," as he called it). With his heart disease, the doctors keep a close watch on him, and monitor his blood often. When riding the little bus, Jay waited for hours to return home (until the shopping was done and the errands were taken care of) which made for a very long, tiring day. He is on oxygen now as he also suffers with lung problems, just as our mother did.

I'm not sure I would be as strong as he's been if I were in his place. Most people probably don't know of the struggles he faces daily, but West Virginian's are strong and persevere through rough times.

For those neighbors, or passers-by, which have helped him, I wish I had the opportunity to thank them for their kindness. Living five hundred miles away, I have felt helpless at times, and wished there was something I could do to make his life a little easier.

I told our older brother that Jay didn't have the advantages that he and I have had. Jay couldn't just jump in the car and take off down the road whenever he wanted to. Joe has no idea what it is like to have to depend on someone else for many things in life. This is not Jay's choice. He would like the opportunity to be as independent as we've been; however, his health has prevented that from a very early age. Sometimes we may look around at people with a critical eye, while having no real idea of what's going on inside, or what challenges they face just to survive.

Heading Out On My Own

My high school teachers, especially Mr. Richardson, strongly urged me to go on to college after graduation, and even though I admired and respected him, I wasn't interested in pursuing college at the time. I felt like I'd had enough school for a while.

I decided to take a job in Spencer, the county seat, about 15 miles away. Linda Paxton was already working at the factory after graduation, making wheel covers for cars (not hubcaps – we didn't dare call them hubcaps). I got a job at Norris Industries, too. We soon decided to get an apartment in Spencer and room together. It was much easier than driving back and forth, especially in the winter when we had to travel over snow-covered hills and around slick, icy curves, especially that steep hill between Gandeeville and Speed. And, it seemed a perfect time to start out on our own.

Janet and I had lived side by side near Walton for several years and we were such good friends. It was hard to leave her. I don't think I realized then how betrayed she must have felt when I went away. That's something I regret as she was, and is, a wonderful friend and I missed seeing her as often.

The factory in Spencer proved to be anything but glamorous. We worked on an assembly line doing various jobs, changing from time to time. I remember running a spinner machine. It reminded me of standing in front of the old-fashioned wringer washing machine, minus the wringer. I placed metal parts in the round machine, which had been greased with strong smelling grease, then pushed the buttons so the spinner would "spin" or bind the pieces together, and if you were lucky, they passed inspection. Often times, the machine would sling some of the smelly grease onto our clothes. There was the nicest young man named Dana, who worked in the salvage department at the back of the plant. He took care of the scrap metal (like the ones I ran on the spinner when they didn't turn out right). Dana had a crush on me. I liked him very much, but not in the same way. After breaking his heart for about the tenth time, he brought me a bottle of Ambush perfume, the kind I liked to wear, and the one he had complimented me on. I suppose the perfume was one last try to win me over. The perfume wasn't made by some big ritzy department store name. The morning he brought it to me at work, he noticed the label. It said, oddly enough, "by Dana." That touched his heart, and I felt even worse than ever. I can still see the sadness in his eyes as he handed me the bottle of perfume and walked away. He was such a kind soul.

Sometimes we had to work on the assembly line putting spokes in the fancy wheel covers, like the Cadillac, or in the shipping department making sure the wheel covers were properly shrink-wrapped and then packed into boxes.

Eventually, I transferred to the press department where mostly the men worked running big presses which "pressed-out" the wheel covers into shapes from huge rolls of flat steel. It was very hot in the summer. We had only fans to cool us. It was cold in the winter, especially if you worked near the loading dock where snow blew in when the big doors had to be opened.

While working at the plant, I started having severe chest pains, and Dad encouraged me to see a doctor. He left me a handwritten note one morning, "Honey, the old ticker is nothing to fool around with. I'll pay for a day's work and doctor's fee if you will go wherever we can get you an appointment. Call back on your first break and tell us to go ahead. Love you, Dad." Then he added, "P.S. Probably won't do much first visit, but will set up another appointment (time is more important than money sometimes)." Then as an afterthought, in that humorous way of his when he was always trying to put us at ease, he added, "I've got to get rid of some of my money or buy a new billfold, and I don't want to buy one. Ha."

I did go to a doctor as my dad encouraged me, but the doctor thought I was just having muscle spasms.

Sometimes at the plant, we would sit on the floor out in the long entrance hall during a break. One day while a whole group of us were sitting out there, a mouse ran around the corner past Linda. She screamed, which sent the whole group of guys into an uproar of laughter.

While I was walking through the plant on my way back to my work station one day, a girl named Darla walked up to me and slapped me so hard she nearly knocked me down. Darla was dating another employee who I had gone out with a couple of times, but that was some time before they even met. She was so jealous of me, although I gave her no reason to be. A supervisor came by to break us up (although I was so stunned I hadn't even hit her back). We were both taken to the office and given suspension slips. I was so upset. I went home to Mom and Dad's, crying so hard that I had a splitting headache. Nothing like that had ever happened to me, and I was humiliated that it happened in front of everyone, and devastated that I might lose my job. We belonged to a union, and my grievance went to arbitration, and my job was restored to me, but she lost her job. I saw her in town some time after that, and she apologized to me for what happened.

While living in Spencer and working at the factory, Linda and I rented a couple of different places. One was in a mobile home park owned by a very strict, older woman. She didn't seem to understand that we were young and liked to listen to our stereo; it wasn't as if we were in a rock band or anything, but to her it was taboo.

We found another place. It was an upstairs apartment over a woman's house, with a side entrance. It had a small kitchen and bathroom, two beds – one at the top of the stairs and one at the other end of the apartment, divided only by a chest of drawers. It was small, but we adjusted. The owner offered to let us use her hibachi. I looked at her like she was speaking another language. I had no idea what a hibachi was. She explained that it was a small grill, and we were welcome to use it if we liked.

We worked hard at the factory. On weekends, usually Friday or Saturday night, we liked to go to Parkersburg, the next town large enough to have shopping centers and nice restaurants. Sometimes we went to the city park where we could stroll around the grounds. It was a nice place to meet new people, in an atmosphere where we didn't have to be afraid. It was like the hangout for young people, much like a Dairy Queen or car wash. We often went dancing later in the evenings. One place we went to had a dance floor with one whole wall of mirrors, and it had a strobe light overhead that reflected throughout the room – quite different than anything we were used to.

Tall, dark and handsome may sound cliché, but I've never known the description to be more fitting. My friends and I were sitting at a table when this gorgeous guy walked in. I caught my breath when I saw him. He walked over to our table, leaned down and asked me to dance. I thought I would faint. His name was Roger, and we hit if off from the beginning. He had a mustache; his hair was dark, parted in the middle, and came down about his shoulders. He had dark brown eyes and a beautiful smile. I found out later that he was from Florida, and was working in the area. He asked to see me again, and I gave him directions to our apartment in Spencer.

Roger came all the way from Parkersburg in Wood County to Spencer in Roane County, almost a fifty mile trip, to pick me up one day. We were riding along on rural route 14, traveling back towards Parkersburg, when all of a sudden he stopped the car in the middle of the road and leaned over and kissed me, and then said, "I've wanted to do that ever since we left." We enjoyed being with each other, and had a wonderful time together. Eventually, I took him to meet my parents at Walton.

One evening, I invited Roger to come by our apartment. I was making a nice dinner for him. I waited and waited, but he didn't show up. Not even a phone call. I was devastated. He had vanished, and I couldn't understand why he had left so abruptly. I heard sometime later that he had gone back to Florida to take care of some unfinished business, and then returned back to Spencer later to try to find me, but I had already moved. I never heard from him again.

I worked at the factory in Spencer for about eight years until I was on a temporary layoff, during one of our slow periods. I took a part-time job as a cashier at a grocery store. I worked there for a few months until I found a full-time job at a local bank.

Linda and I moved back home with our parents eventually. Being out on our own wasn't "all that it was cracked up to be" as the saying goes.

Kroger-ing

When I was on a temporary layoff from the factory, I applied for a cashier's job at Kroger in Clendenin, about twelve miles from Walton.

The manager, Mr. Almond, interviewed me and hired me as a part-time cashier. I remember being very nervous. I didn't have any experience; all I'd ever done was make wheel covers for cars. They trained me briefly on a register (without customers), but I was soon put to work doing the real thing. My supervisor said the best way to learn was to just "jump in and do it." Well, that was easier said than done. This was way back when all the groceries were marked with a price tag. We didn't have the luxury of scanners.

My first day running a cash register has stayed with me all these years. I was slow, of course, because I had to look for the price on each item and then key in the amount. If the price tag wasn't on an item, and there wasn't another associate nearby to help us, we had to go to the shelf and look it up for ourselves. There was this one man in particular who came in and found himself in my line, much to his dissatisfaction. By the time he got up to my register, he was fuming. I apologized for the wait and explained that it was my first day on the job. I suppose I should have kept that information to myself because he burst out, "Well, you're never gonna make it like this!"

I felt myself turning several shades of red. I was so embarrassed. There were a lot of customers in the store and all the registers were busy. People all over the front of the store could, and probably did, hear his outburst. It's a wonder I stuck with the job.

I worked with some very nice people, though. One in particular was a pretty blond named Peggy. She was a cashier and front-end supervisor. I enjoyed working with her, and I was glad when we were able to take a break together. And Karen, who worked in the produce department, was very kind and soft-spoken. Karen was also from Walton, and her parents ran the gas station there. And then there was Jeff, who could have stolen the heart of any girl in Clendenin, I imagined. He was a cashier, too, and was very kind to me.

There was a Dairy Queen beside the Kroger parking lot. They had the best chili dogs. They made their own chili, and nobody else around could compete with it. Another place I remember was Shafer's, which was just outside of Clendenin, and a short drive off Interstate 79. Their store was like a gas station/convenience store, but with a grill, too. They made the best potato wedges. My brother Jay told me Shafer's was changed into a 7-Eleven, but they still had potato wedges.

I don't get to go back home to West Virginia as often as I would like, but each time I do, I try to find time to make a trip to Clendenin to get a chili dog and a box of those mouthwatering potato wedges.

Home-Town Bank

After working part-time at Kroger, I found a full-time position at our hometown bank in Walton, and started out in the bookkeeping department. My supervisor's name was also Debbie. She was a young, slender woman with long, dark blond hair. I started out filing copies of statements – pink sheet after pink sheet after pink sheet had to be filed in the little narrow room which was just off the main part of the bookkeeping department. That job got rather monotonous after a while. Mom always said I got bored easily. I was glad when my supervisor let me start reviewing checks. This was something that had to be done every morning. We went through stacks of checks to make sure the dollar amount and the written amount were the same, and also make sure the checks were signed, before they could be processed through the system.

But the incident that really stands out in my mind is the time I offered to come in on a Saturday to help work on a project with the others. I remember Debbie looking at me and chuckling, and in the most polite way she could, she declined my offer, letting me know that I wouldn't be of assistance to them since I wasn't experienced yet. I imagine I would have been more in the way than anything else, but I didn't realize it at the time. In my mind's eye, I can still see that grin on her face as she declined my offer.

Eventually, I moved out front on the teller line where I had interaction with customers. Sometime later, I was given even more responsibility when I started working with Karen, a very nice, patient woman who taught me how to handle CDs and IRAs.

Kentucky Vacation

Dad and Mom took us on a vacation, camping in Kentucky, about three years after my high school graduation. I had never been to Kentucky before.

We visited different state parks. There were horses to ride at Levi Jackson Wilderness Road State Park. Dad, Jay and I decided to ride them on one of the trails. I got "Beth," the very high-spirited horse that definitely had a mind of her own and knew where she wanted to go. I was not used to riding horses, and hadn't been on one since I was little when Dad bought us a pony, Mr. Ed. With Beth, I had to climb up on something to mount her; she was so tall. Dad, on the other hand, got a very tame horse that hung his head and barely moved along. I think we would have been more suited for each other. I can't remember what Jay's horse was like.

We also visited Fort Boonesborough which had been reconstructed as a working fort. When Daniel Boone and his men reached the Kentucky River in April, 1775, they moved to quickly establish this site as Kentucky's second settlement; Harrodsburg being the first, named after James Harrod in 1774. We were able to tour the cabins and watch the people make candles and crafts like they did back in Daniel Boone's day. It gave us an idea of what it was like for pioneers in Kentucky.

We took a paddleboat ride on the Kentucky River. I think it was called the *Dixie Belle*. We had a very knowledgeable guide, who happened to be a cute young man as well, so you can imagine I enjoyed the boat ride very much.

We saw green rolling hills and numerous horse stables as we traveled through Kentucky. It was very beautiful country.

Mom's Hospital Stay

My dad had been diagnosed with cancer and was going through chemotherapy treatments. Mom was very attentive to him. During this time, she also became sick with what people used to refer to as "female problems" – not something people talked about much back then.

Even though Mom didn't want to go in the hospital while Dad was sick, her doctor didn't give her much choice. He said it was crucial she have the operation. Mom had complications after the surgery and developed blood clots. She was very sick – so sick in fact that she didn't even know me when I came to visit her, which hurt me very deeply.

I tried to be the strong one in the family and drive Dad to the hospital, which was about an hour away, so we could visit with Mom. In the meantime, I was also doing the cooking and trying to take care of the house. Mom was in the hospital seventeen days, which seemed like an eternity.

Easter was approaching and Mom was supposed to get out of the hospital soon, so I took on the task of cooking a turkey dinner for the family, my first. As I didn't know anything about giblets, they remained inside the turkey, and the whole thing was baked together. Even though I've been complimented often on my cooking and baking as I got older, the "turkey story" was one that I've never quite been able to live down.

Niagara Falls

While I was working one summer, Mom, Dad and Jay went on vacation in their pickup truck and camper. The first stop was Aunt Louise's in Painesville, Ohio, about three hundred miles away. Mom and Aunt Louise were both very good cooks, and enjoyed cooking and baking together. They had such a good time visiting and reminiscing about old times in West Virginia.

Next, they headed out to Buffalo, New York. There, they found a well-kept campground on the outskirts of the city. There were brochures posted there about Niagara Falls, and they contacted one of the tour bus companies listed. The bus picked them up, and then they were off; next stop, Customs before entering Canada.

They took a boat ride on the *Maid of the Mist*, which took them under the falls; they had to wear rain ponchos to protect them from the spray of the rushing torrents. One of the tourists took a photograph of them in their ponchos, and I still have that.

Mom described the flowers on the Canadian side as absolutely beautiful. The Falls were lit up at night with spotlights in a rainbow of colors, and the fireworks, along with the backdrop of multifaceted hues, were just magnificent.

Beckley Exhibition Coal Mine

My parents, along with my younger brother, Jay, visited Beckley, in southern West Virginia, which is the largest city in Raleigh County, and where its main street features a lovely historic district. Their main destination was to visit the Exhibition Coal Mine. A visit to the Exhibition Coal Mine begins at the company store and museum where tickets are purchased and where visitors may view an extensive collection of mining artifacts and tools, as well as photos and other features of early life in the coal towns.

The main attraction for my family was the actual tour that took them below ground, under the supervision of a tour guide who was a veteran coal miner. They donned their yellow helmets and traveled 1,500 feet below the hillsides of New River Park, where they were carried along the track, riding in a long yellow "man car" from the entrance to the working areas of the coal mine. This tour was a history lesson in coal mining. Mom remembered seeing the walls of rock, then a black vein of coal, another layer of rock, and another vein of coal. They stopped throughout the tour where the guide explained the history of the low-seam coal mining when coal was excavated by hand with picks and shovels.

A coal company provided a unique way of life for West Virginia miners and their families. As most coal mines were not located near established towns, coal companies built their own towns and provided small, inexpensive homes, along with a church and a company store.

Beckley recently completed an extensive renovation of their coal camp. In addition to the mine tour at Beckley, visitors can visit the historical coal camp where the Coal Company House, Superintendent's Home, Pemberton Coal Camp Church, and the Helen Coal Camp School have been restored.

Also, the gift shop has many unique items to commemorate your visit, including West Virginia food products, coal jewelry and figurines, clothing, authentic-looking underground helmets for children, toys and books on mining, and their homemade fudge from the Fudgery.

Mom brought home black bear coal figurines as souvenirs from their day's coal mining exploration.

Wheeling Jamboree

Wheeling is in the northern panhandle of West Virginia, directly across the river from the state of Ohio, and only eleven miles west of Pennsylvania.

The Wheeling Jamboree in Wheeling, West Virginia, is for fans to enjoy both as a theatre audience and as a loyal radio audience.

The Capitol Music Hall hosts the Wheeling Jamboree, and the "Walkway of Stars" includes such names as Marty Robins, Alabama, Loretta Lynn, Johnny Cash, The Statler Brothers, Barbara Mandrell, Brad Paisley and many more. It is the second longest running weekly radio program, behind the Grand Ole Opry.

Wheeling Jamboree was established by a group of dedicated individuals who have preserved this historic show. Patrons in the 1930s paid twenty-five cents for Saturday night concerts to see the stars whose music filled the airwaves, and their hearts.

My parents took my brother Jay to the Wheeling Jamboree, and they enjoyed hearing various performers, including the legendary Charley Pride. I have a photograph of Dad and Jay standing on the sidewalk under the CAPITOLMUSIC HALL sign with WWVA 1170 printed on a smaller sign above it, and WELCOME TO WHEELING HOME OF JAMBOREE USA on a sign underneath.

Chapter 10
From Heartache to Hope

Bubby

My friends and I often went out on a Friday or Saturday night to hear a band play, and we loved to dance. When the disco scene was big, bell-bottom pants and bright colored shirts were in style.

Some years later, I met Johnny a handsome young man from Charleston. We dated for a while. I liked him a lot until I met Bubby, who also knew Johnny.

Bubby owned a boat and a camper, and sometimes we would go to Summersville Lake and camp with another couple and their young daughter. Summersville Lake offers tremendous fishing and boating, with a full service marina. The lake is characterized by steep cliffs, and divers can swim through overhangs. The more adventurous find rock climbing on the cliffs of Summersville Lake quite exhilarating. It has 60 miles of shoreline. The dam is on the Gauley River near the town of Summersville in Nicholas County. On some days of sunshine, when the water is released from numerous valves, the torrents of water shooting from these valves have been known to create a rainbow of colors.

Bubby and I didn't rock climb, but we did enjoy boating on the beautiful water. He had a pretty Chris-Craft boat. It was a brown wooden boat, and it glistened like a new penny in the sunshine. Once, while we were in the boat and I was shoving off from the dock, I forgot I had Bubby's keys in my hand, and I dropped them in the lake, and they didn't have a floater to keep them on the surface. Bubby dove in after them as that was the only set of keys that he had, and everything he owned was on that key ring. He spotted something shiny and grabbed for it, and luckily it was his keys. Probably lucky for me – I can't imagine what the outcome might have been otherwise.

Bubby was a regular at our house. He was tall with dark, wavy hair and brown eyes that twinkled when he smiled, unless you got him riled, and he gave the best hugs. Sometimes he took me to a nice restaurant, and other times we would just stay home, or go for a walk up the hollow from our house. Just being together was what mattered to us, and we could be ourselves with one another. He celebrated special days, like birthdays and Christmas, with us, too.

I still have a picture of me with him and that charming smile; the photo was taken in 1982; ironically the same year that the song, "Truly," by Lionel Richie topped the charts as No. 1 for two weeks in a row. Hearing those lyrics can really take you back.

The Wedding

While I was dating Bubby, Linda met a handsome young man named Chip who lived in Big Chimney, near the garage where Bubby worked. I met Chip's family, too. His mom made the best oatmeal cookies with cream filling.

Eventually, Chip and Linda were to be married, and I was to be her maid of honor. Janet and Linda's friend, Charlotte, from work, were also in the wedding party. We wore long, mint green dresses. They were not the exact same style, but they were all about the same color so they blended nicely. Bubby, as well as Chip's brother, and another friend, wore mint green tuxes with dark green trim. They looked very handsome. Bubby was the best man so he and I walked down the aisle together as we exited the church.

Just before the ceremony, Bubby presented me with a pre-engagement ring which he hoped would please me, but it upset me instead. I wasn't ready for this kind of commitment, and was embarrassed to be put on the spot like that. I accepted the ring as I did not want to cause a scene. After all, it was Linda and Chip's big day.

While we were standing at the altar, and the Wedding March began, I burst into tears as Linda came down the aisle. I had no idea that I would react like that. I was so moved and couldn't quit crying.

Florida Vacation

In April 1983, Bubby and his family were going to Florida to visit his grandmother and Disney World, and he asked me to go with them. I was torn about what to do. My dad had been sick with cancer, and I was afraid to go so far away. Dad gave me some extra money to fly home if he got worse and encouraged me to go.

We went to Florida in a pickup truck and camper with his family – nephews and all – about a dozen of us, if I remember correctly.

While in Florida, we did some sightseeing. Bubby took me to Weeki Wachee Springs State Park where we saw a mermaid show. It was exciting to watch them underwater. We went to a small beach one day where I used what I thought was suntan oil "with" sunscreen, but I found out at the end of the day that there must have been little, if any, sunscreen in that suntan oil. I looked like a lobster, and felt like a broiled one. Needless to say, getting around was not easy for the rest of the trip.

We did make it over to Disney World one day, but one day is just not nearly enough time to spend there, especially if it's during Spring Break. The long lines were everywhere. One ride that I especially enjoyed was *20,000 Leagues Under the Sea.*

The ride back home seemed endless. I think it took us about 15 hours to get back to West Virginia.

Heart Attack

I was only back from my Florida vacation with Bubby's family about two weeks when my dad had a heart attack. It was a Monday afternoon.

My oldest brother left the day before to go back into the Navy. He was to be stationed in Maine. He had already served ten years, and we rarely saw him during that time. He did not re-enlist right after his ten years were up. He lived in Washington state for a while. Our dad wrote him and asked him to come home. I think my brother may have resented that request at the time as he had already started a new life out there.

Joe was home for a few months, but never found a job he liked, so he decided to re-enlist. He was leaving that Sunday to go to Maine. He and our dad were out in the front yard and I believe Dad asked him, "Aren't you going to tell me goodbye? I may never see you again."

They hugged. That was something I don't remember ever seeing them do.

The next day, Dad had his heart attack. He got up that afternoon from a nap and went up to the cellar building to work on a lawn mower. He liked to tinker with things. He was very handy around the house. My younger brother was with him. He said Dad dropped the screwdriver he was using on the lawn mower and said, "I'm dying."

By the time we got to him, his eyes were glazed over.

I can still see those blue eyes in my mind, even today.

We called for help and tried to do CPR, even though we weren't trained. Paramedics came and he was taken by ambulance to the hospital in Spencer. He died in the emergency room that afternoon. Mom had asked me to call Grandma Maze, her mom, and she came to the hospital. They put us in a room to wait while they tried to revive him. The doctor came in shaking his head. Dad's heart was so weak from the cancer treatments. This was his second heart attack.

Jay stayed at the house to make phone calls. He called Uncle Denzil (Dad's brother, who only lived about a half hour from us because he was working away from home) to let him know we were at Spencer. I lived at home with Mom and Dad and my younger brother at the time.

As Mom and I left Spencer, we met Denzil on his way there. We stopped the car and I got out and talked to him. I thought he knew we lost Dad, but he only knew he had the attack. I could tell by the shocked look on his face. I hated the way I broke it to him, but I didn't know.

Since Joe was on his way to Maine, and we didn't have any idea when he would arrive, we had to contact the police to be on the lookout for him. They put out an APB (all-points bulletin). However, Joe had reached the Navy base earlier in the week than expected, but had not checked in, since he was not due for duty yet. When he did check in, his commanding officer had to break the news to him that his father had passed away. Joe made the trip back home to West Virginia. We had to wait until Saturday to have the funeral, and that was one of the longest weeks of our lives.

We were all devastated. Mom cried endlessly, and I felt so bad for her. It was days before we could eat or drink anything.

Going to the funeral home to make arrangements and picking out the casket was one of the hardest things we'd ever done.

So many people came to the funeral home to express their sympathy. At the end of visitation the night before the funeral, after everyone except the family had left, I thought it would be the last time that I would see my dad, and I couldn't bear the thought. I can remember crying out, "Daddy! Daddy!" as they pulled me away from the casket. I also remember the sadness in the eyes of one of my uncles as he heard me cry out.

We were so torn up that I didn't even know what the preacher said at the funeral. I do remember one song they played; it was "Peace in the Valley."

I was twenty-five at the time, but in my heart I was still daddy's little girl. He used to tease me all the time by saying, "You're the best little girl I've got," then he would laugh and say, "You're the only little girl I've got." That was a special thing between us.

Dad had suffered a lot with cancer and heart problems those last few years. I wish I could have done more for him. I wish I'd been more mature and responsible to have been able to help my mom more. While he was very sick, he had a serious talk with us. I believe he was truly repentant. He asked us to remember the good times, and I do. I don't dwell on the past. He told my mom in a private conversation she was going to be a young widow, and he was right. He died in 1983, three months before his fiftieth birthday, and Mom was only forty-six at the time.

Before he passed away, he gave us children a thank you card addressed "To: My children, Joe, Deborah, Jay" and it read, "Thank you for everything you have done and given me while I have been sick. Love all you, Dad."

He had known he was sick for some time, and had written each of us children a personal letter about two years before he died. He hid them in the top of his closet, and we didn't know anything about them until after he passed away. Each letter had our name on it and the words "to be opened after." I cherish the letter Dad wrote to me in his own handwriting, and I'm sure my brothers do, too. We've never read each other's letters, or even asked. It's a personal thing, and it has been a comfort to me since he's been gone.

Break Up

Bubby still came to see me after Dad passed away. Bubby wanted to be there for me, but he just didn't seem to know how. I needed some time to myself, time to heal. I believe he thought I could just go on as before. Maybe I was moody, but I was grieving. I couldn't close my eyes for the longest time without seeing Dad's glazed eyes as he knelt there in the cellar building on that awful day, or see him in the casket with his hands folded across his chest.

Bubby and I quarreled one day when he came to see me, and I let him leave. I guess we were both too stubborn to see the other's side of things. I regretted later that we hadn't patched things up.

Woodstove & Lumberjacks

After my dad passed away, our free gas was taken away from us, by the widow of the man who had sold us the house. We had to have a woodstove put in for heating. We had to buy the stove, the pipe, and everything necessary for the connections.

A few times, we had to get somebody to cut a truckload of wood for us, which was by no means inexpensive, but most of the time Mom and Jay brought the wood in. I don't mean that they just brought it in from outside. I mean they *really* brought it in – from the woods. Dad had taught Mom how to drive his brown Chevy 4-wheel drive pickup before he passed away. Mom drove the pickup, and she and Jay went up the steep hills above our house and out the ridge to get in firewood. They took a chain saw for cutting down the trees and trimming them. After choosing a tree, they had to determine in which direction they wanted it to fall, and pick a spot where they could take cover when it fell. They had to do what was known as "limbing" the fallen tree by removing the branches. They tackled the small branches first with an ax, which sliced through the branches up to an inch thick or so. When they removed the smaller branches and pulled them away from the trunk, they fired up the chain saw again and cut the larger branches off in sections that could be pulled clear and cut later. Then, they had to saw the trunk into chunks. This is where the serious cutting began as they had to know how long a stick of wood the stove would hold (and with our stove, Mom remembered that it was thirteen inches), and then they sawed the lengths accordingly. If the trunk or large branch was resting on the ground, they didn't cut it all the way through. Instead, they made a series of partial cuts at the desired firewood-length, and then they rolled the trunk or branch over to complete the cut. Once the lengths were cut, they were ready to be loaded on the pickup.

Mom said that sometimes Grandma Maze would come down and go in the woods with them and help with the loading and unloading. I worked full-time, and I don't remember being a part of the lumberjack business.

After several hours of work in the woods, they started back down the steep, treacherous, muddy roads, slipping and sliding, and praying they wouldn't land over the hill somewhere with the pickup truck of wood on top of them. When they made it back home, they unloaded the truck, and then the wood was ready for Jay to split into firewood.

Oak and hickory were hardwood and burned longer than other wood, like pine. Jay's tools for splitting wood were an ax, a splitting maul, and a couple of wedges. The ax worked on logs if they weren't too big, or if he was splitting kindling. For the heavier and more gnarled wood, he used a splitting maul. The blade on the maul looked like an ax on one end and a sledgehammer on the other. This took a lot of elbow grease, but he got plenty of practice, and his swing became more comfortable and accurate over time.

When Jay finished cutting the firewood, they had to stack as much as they could on the back porch, and the rest they stacked in the yard. The fresh cut trees needed to dry out or season so they kept as much wood as possible covered; the wood that was stacked in the yard was covered with a tarp to protect it from the worst of the harsh winter weather.

Mom and Jay made many trips back on the hill bringing in the wood, which was not only essential to heat our home, but also provided a means for cooking some of our meals. We had bought an electric cook stove, second-hand, for most of the cooking after the free gas was gone, but Mom had a big Corning glass pot that she cooked beans and soups on top of the woodstove in the living room.

The woodstove heated our downstairs, but it still got very cold upstairs. At bedtime, we warmed ourselves near the stove before hurrying into our beds, under a pile of quilts and comforters. Sometimes we had so many covers on our bed that we could hardly turn over during the night.

Secretarial College

About three years after Dad passed away, and while I was working at our local bank, a friend of mine, Deanna, suggested I go back to school. She recommended I keep my current job and go to school at night. She attended a college in Charleston, about an hour away. At first, I didn't think I could do that. Go back to school after being out for ten years? It was 1986, after all.

Deanna explained to me that it would open doors for me that otherwise might remain closed. Eventually, I decided to check it out. I applied for student loans at the college and was approved.

I signed up for a year of Secretarial Science in which I should receive a diploma upon completion. Courses included computer, which I had never had any experience with, transcription, speed writing (similar to shorthand), business English and business math, and others.

I was able to ride with Deanna to class. I worked fulltime during the day and went to classes four nights a week. Homework kept me busy on weekends and every spare moment I could get during the week.

My Speed Writing teacher, who worked for an attorney during the day and taught classes at night, came to class every day crying because her boss always said something to hurt her feelings. I was doing very well in her class. One evening she came in and told me she had found another job (working for the state, I believe), and she wanted me to fill her position at the attorney's office. I couldn't believe it at first, and told her so. I reminded her of how miserable she told us she was there. She said it would be good experience for me.

The attorney's office was just down the street from the school. I finally decided to take her advice and apply. I got the job. She came by one day (on a Saturday, I think) and showed me a little bit about her job and the word processor she used to type all the legal documents and letters on. There was no way to learn all I needed to know in one day. When I started the job, I felt as if I had been thrown to the wolves, and wondered what I had gotten myself into. I had to basically teach myself the job, and it was no easy task. I bought a small car so I could drive to work and go to classes at night.

It turned out that the attorney used tapes and a Dictaphone; there was no use for the speed writing I had learned.

There were about five other attorneys in that building who rented office space from my boss. I typed up invoices for rent each month and distributed them.

There was one secretary who had a computer – not an antique word processor like I used. I remember hearing her fingers fly across the keyboard. She said her boss was very good to work for. I remember she detested country music. She came to work one morning laughing and trying to tell me about a song she had heard on the radio that morning. She said that she about died laughing when she heard the lyrics, "I just cut myself on a piece of your broken heart." She thought that was so ridiculous.

There was another secretary who rode her motorcycle to work and parked it out back, in the alley. She would come through the back door, often wearing boots and a red bandana tied around her head. She worked for two or three attorneys in the office. She wasn't the easiest person to get used to talking to.

There was a basement in our office building. My boss warned me never to go down there, but he often went. I always wondered what was so mysterious about it, but I didn't dare ask.

There was a lot of tension there. I don't think everyone got along very well. The others seemed uncomfortable when my boss was there, and more lighthearted when he wasn't.

I worked for the attorney for some time until I couldn't take it any longer. My boss was very rough-talking and had very little patience. I could see why my teacher left there crying so often. Eventually, I resigned, too.

I finished my year of classes, making the dean's list with a GPA of 4.0 for the entire year. I'm amazed that I was able to do that with all the transition. There was a graduation ceremony held at the Holiday Inn Charleston House where I received my Diploma. Mom, my brother Jay, and some of our friends went with us. It was a very nice ceremony, and we had a good meal afterward to celebrate.

The Young Preacher

When we lived at Walton, I started attending a little, white church about a mile from our house. There was a nice grandmother who lived out the lane from the church. Her daughters had both married and were living in Nitro, below Charleston, with their husbands. Each had a child, one had a son whose name was Todd, and the other had a daughter, Shawn. The families came home on the weekends to be with the mother/grandmother and to attend church.

Todd and I were comfortable calling each other brother/sister. As a matter of fact, I even thought of his mother as a "second mother." We were close for several years.

Todd talked me into typing a term paper for him once. He loaned me his typewriter, which had a correction cartridge that you had to slide in and out of the typewriter every time you wanted to correct a mistake. I did the typing in the office of the basement of the church. I think I nearly wore out that correction cartridge, but finally finished the paper for him.

He started dating a girl named Debbie. He told me about her as if he was talking to an older sister. She went to a Pentecostal church, and her pastor was a very good friend of Todd's. Todd went to a holiness church, but he didn't understand all their Pentecostal beliefs.

He had a love for radio broadcasting, and he found a job in the Charleston area. Sometimes, they would send him out on live remote broadcasts. He invited me to one of these, which was being held at a steakhouse on the outskirts of Charleston. I guess he thought I was listening to the broadcast in my car on the way to the restaurant because when I arrived, he stuck a microphone in my face and asked me, "What's the magic word?" Of course I was dumbfounded as he had caught me off guard. I tried to push the microphone away, but he insisted, and asked the question again. We were not on television, so no one could see my expression other than the people in the restaurant, but I realized his radio audience was waiting for an answer, and he wouldn't budge. I didn't have any idea what he was talking about, so I said the first thing that popped into my mind – "sirloin steak."

Todd laughed. He found my uneasiness amusing. Holding a microphone might have been second nature to him, but definitely not to me, and I haven't cared for them since.

Todd and I began to see each other more often. It seemed to happen subtly. Our brother/sister friendship grew into something more. He asked me out to his grandmother's – "Granny's" – after church. Once, he asked me to go to the Pizza Hut at Spencer, on some pretense of discussing a typing project he had in mind for me. We ate a whole pizza and talked and talked, but I don't think we discussed anything about typing.

I was seeing Todd when I was in my late twenties, and while I was going to night school, where I was taking secretarial classes. I worked in Charleston and went to class at night and often went to see him later, which was in the opposite direction of home. Sometimes I would drive to their house in Nitro, and sometimes he would meet me in Charleston. Walking around the Capitol building at night was one of our favorite romantic places to spend time. I look back now and wonder how I kept such a busy schedule. I often drove home at night on the interstate so sleepy that I could hardly hold my eyes open. One night I was so sleepy that I had to pull off on the side of the road and rest for a little bit. I knew it wasn't safe to pull over by myself, but it wasn't safe driving that sleepy either. I had just tilted my seat back to rest a few minutes when an awful crash hit my car. Someone had driven by and thrown a beer bottle through my back glass and it landed in the front floorboard. I sat up and just caught a glimpse of a pickup driving on. They might not have known that I was even in the car at the time. If I hadn't tilted my seat back, I might have been badly hurt by the force of the bottle that came through the glass, or from the broken glass itself. I pulled off the interstate and drove to the nearest police station to report the incident, but of course as the drivers were long gone, they said there wasn't anything they could do.

Todd felt the calling to be a preacher. I went with him and his family to different churches where he would be invited to preach. He was a soft-spoken, good-natured, all-around kind of guy. But when he started preaching, and the anointing fell on him, it would make you sit up and take notice. I was very proud of him.

Once, when we were going out on a date, he wanted to stop by his aunt's house for a minute. I waited for him in the car. When he came back to the car, he leaned over and kissed me. I said, "You had a chocolate chip cookie, and a homemade one at that." He got so tickled at me. He couldn't believe that I knew exactly what he had eaten – just by a kiss. I was trying to lose weight and lay off sweets, but I guess you could say that I had a keen taste – and nose – for food, like a bloodhound.

Todd and I visited Blennerhassett Island Historical State Park in Parkersburg, West Virginia, one Saturday evening and took a sternwheeler ride on the Ohio River. The sunset that evening was breathtaking and so romantic. Anyone planning a trip to Blennerhassett Island may want to allow at least three hours enjoying all it has to offer. In addition to the sternwheeler ride, they offer a horse-drawn wagon ride, and tours of the mansion and gift shop, or you may want to take a self-guided walking tour to explore the island.

Todd was offered the pastorate at a small church in East Bank. I went with him and met the people there. They had a parsonage nearby for the pastor, and Todd stayed there on Sundays. I would go down Sunday morning to church and then stay at the parsonage until time for the evening service. Some of the neighbors (that didn't even attend that church) thought it was inappropriate for the pastor's girlfriend to be there, since we were not married. The members of the church brought this to Todd's attention, which put him in an awkward position, so I quit going to the parsonage. This was about a hundred mile round trip for me, and I couldn't make two trips there in one day, so I didn't get to attend church with him as often. This put a strain on our relationship, to say the least.

We did continue to see each other and we became serious. I had really hoped for an engagement ring one Christmas. We went shopping in the mall and looked in the jewelry store windows. I picked out one that I really liked, but it was costly.

Just before Christmas, Todd came to my house with a little package for me. When I opened it, he could tell by my expression that I was disappointed.

I was just so shocked. It was a small, diamond ring, but nothing like the one I had my heart set on. He thought I just wanted a diamond for Christmas, and went to great lengths to make that possible. It hurt him deeply. I hadn't allowed myself to really believe that I would get a ring that Christmas, even though I had secretly hoped for it. I wanted to accept the ring, but it was sometime before he could forgive me. Eventually, we broke up. This in itself was hard enough, but not having my "other mother" in my life anymore was equally hard, as I loved her, too.

Literary Giants of WV

Pearl S. Buck's parents were missionaries, and although Pearl was born in Hillsboro, in Pocahontas County, West Virginia, she spent much of her life in China. She won the Pulitzer Prize in 1932 for her book, *The Good Earth*, and was the first American woman to win the Nobel Prize for Literature in 1938. *The Good Earth* continues to appear in many United States high school reading lists. The Pearl S. Buck Birthplace is a restored farmhouse, turned into a museum, where guided tours lead you through rooms of original furniture and memorabilia, Pearl Buck Stamps, and other souvenirs.

Catherine Marshall, though born in Tennessee, lived in Keyser, West Virginia in Mineral County for ten years, and graduated from Keyser High School. Her novel, *Christy,* was inspired by her mother's journey, teaching children in the mountains of Tennessee. *Christy* was later turned into a television series starring Kellie Martin.

The first poet laureate of West Virginia was Karl Myers, who overcame tremendous physical challenges. He was born in Tucker County, and was appointed poet laureate by the governor, as were all poet laureates. The current Poet Laureate of West Virginia is Irene McKinney of Belington, a West Virginia Wesleyan professor.

I enjoy poetry very much and have been writing for some time now, more seriously over the past year and a half. Some of my poems have been published in magazines and online journals, and I won an Honorable Mention in 2010.

"A Conversation with Irene McKinney" first aired in September 2005 on the program "Outlook" on West Virginia PBS. This interview has been posted on YouTube, and I was able to enjoy it, as it portrays Ms. McKinney as a very down-to-earth person and one you could sit and talk to for hours. I loved hearing her read some of her own work, and I was able to get a glimpse of her home and the hills surrounding it.

French Creek Game Farm

Leaving Walton, taking Route 119 toward Clendenin and picking up Interstate 79 toward Clarksburg, begins a journey of unforgettable wonders. Following I-79 to the Flatwoods exit, we begin our adventure through these winding roads of West Virginia. Following Route 19 at Flatwoods to Route 4 and then to Route 20, we eventually end up at French Creek.

We've been to French Creek Game Farm on various trips over the years, but since 1986 the facility has changed, for the better. We were used to seeing wild animals in caged exhibits, but the new facility has been renovated to display each animal in its natural habitat. This lets us, the public, get a more realistic view of the state's wildlife.

The new facility is called West Virginia State Wildlife Center. We can now view the wildlife by walking through the woods on a paved trail, which is over a mile long around the animal exhibits. They're out in the woods in this natural habitat where we can see them while walking along this shaded walkway that has a small pond and rest area.

Black bears, mountain lions, bobcats, coyotes, white-tailed deer, as well as small animals and birds, make up this day's exciting adventure. The bison and elk have acres of grass to roam, and the river otters can be viewed, both above and below the water's surface, exhibiting their amazing swimming abilities.

There is a picnic area, fishing pond, and a gift shop with refreshments. Also available for purchase are souvenirs to commemorate the day's breathtaking excursion.

Uncle Blaine

I remember Uncle Blaine as being tall with dark brown hair and brown eyes, and a boyish grin, no matter how old he got. He was Mom's brother, the youngest of the Maze children. As an adult, he lived at Phillip's Run, a few miles above Grantsville in Calhoun County.

Blaine Maze had a lot of friends, and would often invite some of his buddies to go hunting in the hollow and hills behind his house in deer season. He had a back porch where it was shaded and cool, and an ideal place to sit and visit after a long day in the woods. Uncle Blaine was a good cook, of which his friends and family could attest.

He worked for B & F Goodrich in Grantsville for several years, but once their new plant opened in Spencer in Roane County, he transferred there, driving back and forth to work, about an hour away. They also had a plant in Arizona, and he was asked to go out there and work for a while. His experience as an engineer was welcomed.

When Blaine was scheduled to come back from Arizona, he called his good friend, Rick, also of Grantsville, and asked him to meet his plane at the airport in Parkersburg. You would have to know the history behind Rick and Blaine's friendship to imagine the following, as they were always playing tricks on each other. Adults as they may have been, the boyish charm and mischievousness were still there. Rick decided to give Blaine a big surprise when they arrived at the airport. They both knew a local woman whose "elevator didn't quite make it to the top floor." Rick got her all dressed up in a wild-print dress, a straw hat and clodhopper-looking shoes, tied tin cans to his convertible and headed out to Parkersburg. It sort of reminds me of the Clampet family on the Beverly Hillbillies, even before they left the hills. I would have liked to have seen the look on Uncle Blaine's face when he stepped off that plane! I imagine Rick got paid back sooner or later, as Blaine wasn't without a few tricks of his own up his sleeve.

Blaine looked awfully young to be a grandpa, but every summer he took a week's vacation and he and his grandson, Matthew, went fishing and camping down by the river, about a mile below Grandma Maze's. Matthew was a little redheaded boy with freckles, who thought the world of his grandpa. Matthew's father and mother had separated, and Blaine took Matthew in, under his wing, you might say.

Blaine was no stranger to a campfire, and had no qualms about cooking many of the same things he did at home in his own kitchen. Mom remembered him making biscuits and cornbread, fried potatoes, and pinto beans. He had cast iron skillets and kettles, and cooked over wood or charcoal. For his oven, he would get a big kettle and place his biscuits or cornbread batter in it; place charcoals underneath it; place the lid on the kettle; and then place more charcoals on top of the lid; this distributed the heat evenly, giving it an oven effect. Blaine and Matthew had several visitors when suppertime came around. They might have some of their friends stop by, and always some of the family. Grandma Maze loved to go down to the river and join them; Blaine's younger daughter Ann and her husband, Dave, would come by, and Mom and Jay would drive up from Walton to join them. Cooking outdoors always gave everyone a hearty appetite, as if there was something in the air. They sat around the campfire, enjoying the meals, telling stories and reminiscing about younger days.

Uncle Blaine was only in his fifties when he passed away. He had been sick with cancer for some time. Mom was one of the family members who stayed with him near the end, and she was with him when he passed away on Christmas morning, 1997. He is missed by many loved ones and friends alike.

Mary Kay Representative

After I left the attorney's office, and while I was between jobs, I was approached by a Mary Kay Cosmetics Representative who offered me a chance to be my own boss.

She was the wife of a previous co-worker. When she told me about all the benefits Mary Kay Cosmetics had to offer (the cars, the jewels, and the trips), it did sound appealing.

She acted as a mentor while I tried to get my business off the ground. I ordered my skin care kit and contacted my friends to offer them a skin care class. Mary Kay was all about taking good care of your skin – not just about makeup.

My mentor stocked me with supplies from her inventory until I had obtained enough skin care orders to place an order to the company. We had meetings at our district manager's home in Charleston, and I rode to these meetings with her. I found out that it was just as important to recruit new consultants as it was to sell the products. If we made new recruits, a percentage of what they sold would be credited to us. There were points to strive for, and prizes to be won. I had been working so hard. One week, I thought I had placed the biggest company order, and was looking forward to hearing my name announced at our meeting that night. However, what I found out was that my mentor had placed an order exactly ten dollars larger than mine. I didn't realize when she had called me earlier that same day why she needed to know the *exact* dollar amount of the order I was placing, but I certainly found out that night. I felt so betrayed, and if I'd had another way home, I would have taken it.

I suppose this business could be rewarding if you had the funds to amply stock your shelves when you first started out; that way you wouldn't have to keep a client waiting when they needed something. From my experience, most women will buy if you have it in stock, but if they have to wait for it, even if it's only a couple weeks, you've just lost their interest. Unfortunately, I was struggling with having enough funds to place orders from one skin class to another. I realized, too late, that this wasn't for me. I couldn't cut someone else's throat just to come out on top.

Mr. and Mrs. J

Mrs. J., who lived in Walton with her husband who had Alzheimer's, and being at wits end on how to handle the situation, called my mom up one day and asked her if she would consider helping her with her husband.

At first, all she asked of Mom was to help keep an eye on her husband who had a habit of wandering off when she wasn't looking. She couldn't keep up with her house and her husband at the same time. Her list increased steadily over time, and Mom found herself fixing their meals and helping with other household chores, including the laundry and vacuuming the carpets. Mr. J. loved chocolate pie, and his wife asked Mom to bake him one once in a while, which she did.

They were well-to-do people but you wouldn't know it by their actions. Mrs. J. wouldn't let Mom turn the air conditioner up enough to be comfortable. She kept it at least 80 degrees.

One morning, when Mom showed up at their house, Mrs. J. asked for help with cleaning out the basement. Thinking that she planned to stay down there and help her, Mom began the monumental task of making some sort of order out of the chaos. When she looked around to ask Mrs. J. where she wanted something, she realized she was alone. Mrs. J. had made her way back upstairs and was relaxing in her sitting room, watching television. Mom continued with dusting the jars of canned goods on the shelves, scrubbing the cement floor, organizing boxes and odds and ends that had been lying helter-skelter around the room.

Mom was washing dishes at the kitchen sink one morning, where she could see all the way through the house, to the front door. When she glanced around, she saw that the door was open, and Mr. J. was across the highway. He was standing in the yard at the library, talking to someone. It scared Mom to realize he had crossed the highway and could have been hurt, or even killed. She tore out of the house and across the road, and guided him safely home.

Mrs. J. asked her husband if he would like for Mom to cut his fingernails one day, and he replied that he did. Mrs. J. whispered to her, "Ask him for a tip." Mom didn't know that she was being set up, so she asked him. Laughing, he replied, "I'll tip you right off that bridge down there."

Sometimes his mind would come to him, and he'd be laughing and talking, and the next thing they knew he'd be in the kitchen gathering up the sharp kitchen knives. He took them in the living room and hid them under the cushions of his chair. Mom said it was so sad to see him that way, so afraid. This disease was heartbreaking.

Mom only stayed during the day, but Mrs. J. would tell her how he would get up at night, unlock the door, and wander off sometimes. She would have to get up and go hunt for him before he hurt himself. They lived near the river, and he could easily have fallen in. One night, after Mom had gone home, Mrs. J. called her and pleaded with her to come back and help her find him. He had wandered off down through the bottom. He was trying to run away.

They had a winter home in Florida, and Mrs. J. did her best to talk Mom into driving them to Florida one year. Mom hardly drove more than an hour from home, and that was usually to Charleston for doctor's appointments. She couldn't imagine tackling a trip like that, and with an Alzheimer's patient who was always trying to escape!

Eventually, taking care of her husband at home became more than Mrs. J. and Mom together could handle. Mrs. J. reluctantly placed her husband in a nursing home in Spencer, about fourteen or fifteen miles away. As she didn't drive, she called Mom about once a week and asked her to take her to see her husband. She would have Mom stop at the McDonald's, and she would treat her to a biscuit and cup of coffee, and that became their weekly outing for some time.

The Vision

Going through the loss of my father was very hard on us, especially since we weren't going to church at the time, and didn't have our faith to carry us through. I am so thankful now that there were others who were praying for us. We ran into a woman in Spencer one day after the funeral who asked us how we were getting along. She encouraged us to put our faith in God and let Him be our strength.

Sometime later, I did get back into church and found out what I really knew all the time – what that woman said was true – we needed to let the Lord help us through our sorrow.

One day the preacher from the church came by to visit my mom. She was very bitter at the time – she had lost Dad at an early age – and she told me that she wasn't going back to church. The day the preacher came by, she went into the laundry room to avoid him. He was persistent, however, and waited until I could persuade her to come out.

He prayed with us that day. My mom closed her eyes during that prayer, and she told us later that she had seen a vision of my dad, smiling radiantly, with a glow around him; there were beautiful flowers, and it looked like the most beautiful place she had ever seen. She knew that she'd had a vision of my dad in heaven. We had always wondered if he had made it. He was never a church-going man, but he definitely was a changed man during those latter years. No one really knows what goes on between a person and their Maker during those last moments of life.

My mom was reassured that Dad had made it to heaven, and this was a turning point in her life. She did go to church that following Sunday and rededicated her life to the Lord. She has never regretted it for a day.

West Virginia, Wild & Wonderful

West Virginia, its nickname is "Mountain State," but I'll always remember it by the nickname I grew up with – "Almost Heaven, West Virginia."

The rhododendron (also known as Big Laurel) is the state flower – it has large dark evergreen leaves and delicate pale pink or white blossoms; the cardinal is the state bird (also known as red bird, which is especially beautiful against a backdrop of snow in the winter).

The black bear is the state animal; the monarch is the state butterfly; the golden delicious apple is the state fruit; and the sugar maple is the state tree. Its leaves are breathtaking in autumn.

The airport at Charleston was known as Kanawha Airport until October 1985 when it changed its name to Yeager Airport to honor Brigadier General Charles E. "Chuck" Yeager. He was born in Myra, West Virginia, in Lincoln County, and graduated from Hamlin High School. Chuck Yeager was widely considered the first pilot to travel faster than the speed of sound. He broke the sound barrier October 14, 1947.

The capital, and largest city, is Charleston in Kanawha County. The Kanawha River meanders through the valley and mountains surrounding Charleston. Barges can be seen transporting coal on the river. The front of the Capitol building, with its magnificent gold dome, faces the river. Capitol tours and tours of the Governor's Mansion are available for guests and school groups by calling the Cultural Center. We were taken on a tour of the Capitol when we were students in high school. The grand Capitol building features interior details like marble walls and a magnificent imported crystal chandelier. The Corinthian columns made of limestone line both the front and back porticos of the main Capitol building. The west or center balcony of the House Chamber is designated the member's gallery and reserved for guests of members of the House of Delegates, while the north and south galleries are open to the public to view the daily business of the House of Delegates. I recall sitting in the balcony, overlooking the delegates, when I was a student at Walton and had the privilege of touring our Capitol. The grounds have several statues including those of Abraham Lincoln and Stonewall Jackson. Fountains are lit up at night casting reflected images, as I've noticed as an adult, while taking romantic strolls around the grounds.

The State Seal of West Virginia bears the motto in Latin "Montani Simper Liberi" which means "Mountaineers Are Always Free." The seal displays a rock in the middle with the date of admission to the Union, June 20, 1863; a farmer stands on one side of the rock and a miner on the other. Mountaineers are traditionally very independent, hard workers, have pride in their heritage, and in the natural resources of their state, they have survived for generations by farming and preserving enough to see their families through the harsh winters, and have a love for family and a keen sense of loyalty to neighbors, helping out one another in time of need, a quality which has proved sufficient to preserve their way of life in the hills.

Where Are They Now?

My younger brother, Jay, and his wife, Mary, still live at Walton. Jay has always loved to hunt, especially squirrel hunting, just like our dad did. He hunted in the woods above his house until his health prevented it a few years ago. He can still see the deer in the woods just above his house, without leaving his property. He and Mary have raised goats, chickens, ducks, and geese on their land at Walton, but they are now content with their two companions – a boxer and a poodle.

My older brother, Joe, married and when he retired from the Navy, he and his wife, Betty, moved to the green rolling hills of Tennessee. He is a truck driver now and travels cross-country. He's on the wide open road now, and sees the country from a different viewpoint than when he was sailing on the open seas.

Aunt Louise lives in Ohio, not too far from her daughter, Sheila, and her husband, Chuck. One of her granddaughters also lives in Ohio; the other one recently moved to Virginia, but spent some time in Alaska with her husband who is in the service.

Aunt Lyla and Uncle Joe still live in Nutter Fort, West Virginia, near Clarksburg. Their son, Jimmy, lives in Florida and has two children. Jimmy works as a compassionate nurse and is also a talented hairdresser.

Uncle Denzil Richard, who is in his eighties now, resides in Heartland of Clarksburg, near Aunt Lyla, who looks after him and takes care of all his business affairs.

Grandma Maze passed away in January 2010 of pneumonia at age 94. She had been residing in a nursing home in Ohio about a year before she passed away, as my aunt and uncle moved back to Ohio from South Carolina, and they took Grandma with them so she could be near them.

Grandma Richard passed away in 1987 at age 87, four years after my dad passed away. Grandma had a hole in her lung, and had been in and out of the hospital numerous times during the last months of her life. I was 29 at the time and living at Walton. Just before she passed away, I felt an urgency to go visit her in the hospital in Morgantown, almost one hundred and fifty miles away. I'm so thankful I did. That was the last time I saw my Grandma Richard alive.

It seemed that no matter how old I got, Grandma Richard always looked forward to our visits when we went home to Munday. I can still picture her in her kitchen, making pot roast, mashed potatoes, and homemade bread, as only she could make it. The aromas from her kitchen were wonderful. I remember sitting on the front porch and thinking to myself, "This really is like being in a different world." It was so remote that it was almost as if the outside world didn't exist. It was so quiet and peaceful there. I picture Grandma running toward us with open arms and a big smile on her face – the most wonderful welcome we could receive. I often imagine her welcoming me into heaven the same way.

Mom, Then and Now

As Dad had predicted, Mom became a young widow at age 46 in 1983. For nine years, she struggled to keep things going – changing from free gas to bringing in the wood from the hills to fuel the woodstove, and surviving the harsh winters.

Mom recalls being very lonesome during those nine years as it was the saddest time of her life. She had known my dad for thirty years, and had been married to him for twenty-nine. They had worked side by side, remodeled homes – she could use a hammer or saw just the same as he could – working the land, and raising three children. This is the only life she had known since the tender age of seventeen.

After spending several summer vacations at Myrtle Beach over the years, Mom and I talked about how wonderful it would be to live near the beach as we loved the ocean. Jobs were hard to find in West Virginia, at least ones that paid well. I decided that I wanted to move to the south and did so with a friend in June 1990. Once I arrived in the Myrtle Beach area, we found an unfurnished apartment that appeared much smaller than the two-story farmhouse I had been used to for so many years. The first night sleeping on a thin mattress on the floor, and realizing I was more than 500 miles from home, I asked myself, "What have you done?" I missed Mom so much I could hardly stand it.

I finally convinced Mom to move to South Carolina in January 1992. My brother Jay was getting married, and I went home for the wedding. Mom let Jay and his bride, Mary, move into our farmhouse. The very next morning we left West Virginia to begin the long trip to South Carolina. It was twenty degrees below zero with snow on the ground and snow was still pelting down until we reached Charleston in Kanawha County.

We soon found out that living near the beach was not the same thing as being there on vacation – as being on vacation meant just that – vacating from the normal responsibilities of life for a short time. We were used to being catered to, pampered. But when we moved here, no one made our beds and cleaned up after us; we didn't eat out every single day, and we couldn't leave our cares and worries behind us.

Mom is 74 now and has numerous medical problems including COPD with Emphysema and chronic back pain. It has been a long time since she and I have had a chance to go to the beach even though we only live about thirty-five miles away. I worked for a healthcare organization for almost thirteen years before resigning last year to become full-time caregiver for my mom. I have cherished this time we have had together.

After several years in South Carolina, we found a wonderful church, the Church of God in Mullins. I agree with Mom that our pastor and his wife, the Turners, are the most compassionate people we've ever met. They are there for us, day or night, and have spent numerous hours with us at our home, in the hospital, and at rehab.

Although Mom is no longer able to travel to West Virginia, our memories are steadfast and our hearts long for the hills.

"The West Virginia Hills"

The West Virginia Hills is a State Song of West Virginia. Just as our motto "Mountaineers Are Always Free," this song echoes my heart's song – and the tug at my heart strings when I remember my childhood days, the love of family and togetherness, the realization that we may not have had a lot compared to the world's standards, but we were rich. Rich in love and caring – in parents who worked hard to feed and clothe us, to show us we were loved, maybe not in a demonstrative way, but by the sweat of their brow, and the way they made special times like Christmas magical for us; in grandmothers who loved us, and showed us in little ways that were all their own; in family get-togethers, picnics, and visiting on the front porch; in real friends, not just acquaintances. Rich in simpler living, too – playing games that I wish all children knew about – wading the creek, walking through the woods, picking wildflowers, spending the day with your best friend – no one can put a price tag on that.

"The West Virginia Hills"

VERSE 1:

Oh, the West Virginia hills! How majestic and how grand,
With their summits bathed in glory, Like our Prince Immanuel's Land!
Is it any wonder then, That my heart with rapture thrills,
As I stand once more with loved ones On those West Virginia hills?

CHORUS:

Oh, the hills, beautiful hills, How I love those West Virginia hills!
If o'er sea o'er land I roam, Still I'll think of happy home,
And my friends among the West Virginia Hills.

VERSE 2:

Oh, the West Virginia hills! Where my childhood hours were passed,
Where I often wandered lonely, And the future tried to cast;
Many are our visions bright, Which the future ne'er fulfills;
But how sunny were my daydreams On those West Virginia hills!

VERSE 3:

Oh, the West Virginia hills! How unchang'd they seem to stand,
With their summits pointed skyward To the Great Almighty's Land!
Many changes I can see, Which my heart with sadness fills,
But no changes can be noticed In those West Virginia hills.

VERSE 4:

Oh, the West Virginia hills! I must bid you now adieu.
In my home beyond the mountains I shall ever dream of you;
In the evening time of life, If my Father only wills,
I shall still behold the vision Of those West Virginia hills.

There is Hope

Many changes have taken place in my life. Changes as real as the changes of the seasons: the warmth of summer and gentle breezes; to the briskness of autumn with the colors of the trees in the West Virginia hills – lemon yellow, burnt orange, strawberry red; to the harshness of winter when the trees are bare, and the ponds freeze over; to the thawing of spring with the unfolding of flower petals, and the scampering of young wildlife in the forests – as new life replaces the starkness and loneliness of winter.

I've had my ups and downs, happiness and disappointments, loves and losses, loneliness and renewing of faith – faith in One much higher and wiser than I – One who has created the universe and the people in it, people who have such an impact on our lives, be it good or bad. But one principle I have found to be steadfast: while there is life, there is hope.

Appendix:
Photo Album

George Washington (Wash) Munday, Grandma Rose's Dad (Born 1861)

Anna (Slater) Munday, Grandma Rose's Mother (Born 1868)

Asa Maze, Flora Maze, Grandma Hazel Rose

Mom's first school, the barn and house where Asa & Flora Maze lived (Aunt Betty's family later lived)

Lucille (left), Aunt Annie Amos (middle), 1950

Mom (Naomi Karen Maze)

Clarence Maze Jr, Betty Maze, Naomi Karen (my mom), Roger Maze, Connie Maze

Debbie, Grandma Maze, Jay

Gail, Tom, Linda, and Mark Krugman, Joe, Debbie, and Jay Richard (first cousins) 1965

Grandma Hazel Rose and her flowers (photo developed Jan 1964; probably taken in Summer of 1963)

Grandpa Sampson Rose sitting by the river, just below his house, Sept 1955

Jeff Lahman with Uncle Blaine Maze, Christmas 1986 at Grandma Maze's

Maze Family - Clarence Sr., Blaine, Nona seated; Connie, Naomi Karen, Betty, Clarence Jr. (Roger missing)

Mom, Jay, Debbie and Joe at Grandma Maze's (1963)

Pleasant Valley United Brethren Church, Maze Reunion, 1940's (Church where Mom played piano as a girl)

Sarah (Boice) Rose, Grandpa Samp Rose's Mother (Born 1852)

Clarence Maze, Jr. with John, Marlene, and Tom

Maze Cemetery, out the ridge from Grandma Maze's (cousins Ann Maze, Marsha Krugman with Jay Richard)

Belt Store at Industry, around 1940 (Courtesy of HurHerald.com)

Brooksville School - Where Grandma Maze worked (Courtesy of HurHerald.com)

Calhoun's Famous Schoolhouse Cave - Education in 1818 (Courtesy of HurHerald.com)

Gr. Maze and granddaughter Jenni Lahman, taken on the deck in front of Grandma's cellar, Sept 1991

Joe, Mom, Jay, Debbie, July 1964 (Grandma Richard's house in background, Munday, WV in Wirt County)

Jay and Debbie giving dolls a bath in creek, Munday, WV (footbridge in background), 1968

Dad in our front yard at Munday, 1964 ('57 Chevy in background and footbridge across creek)

Jay washing dishes at Munday, smiling for the camera, 1966

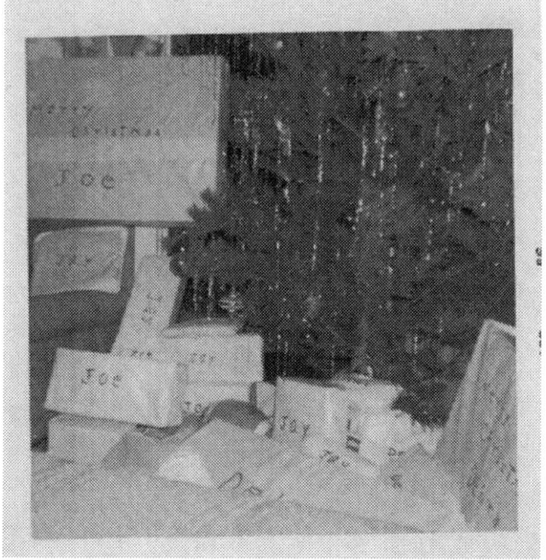

Personalized Christmas presents (Munday, 1965)

Bell School at Munday, WV 1938 (Courtesy of HurHerald.com)

Bell School 1967; Debbie 7th from left; Elaine Toney 5th from left; Jay seated 2nd from left; Ms. Quick, left; Ms. Mills, right

(1968) Middle - Roberta, Pam, Sherry, Debbie R., Fr. LouAnn (white boots), Ms. Quick, left; Ms. Mills, Ms. Underwood, right

Debbie returns to Bell School (all grown up, late 1970s)

Our House at Munday, WV (Wirt County) 1964

Our House at Munday, 1964 (view from hill across the road)

Arlis Richard, age 6 (my dad), 1940

Uncle Jack Mathess (Louise's husband)

Ada Bell Munday, Ellen Bell, Mildred Bell Pettit (Courtesy of Hur Herald.com)

Basil Pepper, Gr. Edna Richard, Thelma Kelly, Gr.Grandpa Omer Pepper, Nina Rogers, Debbie in front, May 29, 1960

Gr. Richard's house, Grandma, Dad (Arlis), Lyla, Denzil, Lester, Louise

Gr. Richard with Jay, Debbie, Jimmy Kopshina, Joe (our front yard at Munday)

Jay, Debbie, Dad and Joe leaning against Dad's Chevy, 1964

Lyla and Joe Kopshina, Easter 1982 (Their home in Clarksburg, WV)

Robert's Store, A Wirt County Landmark (Courtesy of HurHerald.com)

Our house at Walton, before remodeling, 1969

Our house at Walton, after remodeling

Backyard at Walton - Gr. Richard, Gr. Maze (standing), Aunt Louise, Dad and Jay, 1982

Alan Webb, cellar and cellar building in background, Walton 1972

Debbie and Janet before Senior Prom (Walton), 1976

Mr. Mike Richardson, Teacher at Walton High School

Wayne D. (Walton High School)

Though the years rush in
Upon the shores of time,
It's the memories of happy days
That remain to be remembered.

Walton High School, 1976

Graduation 1976, on steps of Walton High School - Harold, Linda, Mary, Janet, and Debbie

Linda Paxton and Chip Hoover's Wedding - Debbie (Maid of Honor), Janet Walker (far left), Bubby Vance (Best Man)

Debbie and Dad, Walton

Dad and Christmas Cookies, playing Chef Tell, Walton

Dad at dress up, Sheik or Shepherd (Walton), 1972

Debbie and Mom (Walton)

Dad and Mom's 29th Anniversary, Feb. 9, 1983 (Last one before Dad passed away in April)

Harry and Levie Walker (Janet's Parents) at our house, Walton

Jay shoveling snow on roof over back porch, Walton

Joe Richard (Navy, Aug. 1977)

About the Author

DEBBIE RICHARD is a native of West Virginia. Born in Parkersburg, she spent her early childhood in the rural community of Munday in Wirt County, and lived near Walton in Roane County during her high school years. Debbie studied Secretarial Science at West Virginia Career College in Charleston where she completed her courses in 1987 with honors. She moved to the South as an adult, following her love of the ocean. After twelve years as a Report Analyst for a healthcare organization, she resigned in March 2009 to become full-time caregiver for her mother, Naomi Karen (Maze) Richard, who grew up near Big Bend in Calhoun County, West Virginia. Debbie's mother passed away in March 2011. Debbie volunteered as an Office Assistant with Mercy Care hospice in Myrtle Beach beginning in July 2011 and later worked as a Finance Assistant with them until December 2012. She recently tested a new computer system for McLeod Loris Seacoast while working as a Secretary in Administration.

Debbie is a member of South Carolina Writers' Workshop and West Virginia Writers, Inc. She is the recipient of an Honorable Mention in the 2010 *Joyful!* Poetry Contest, and her poems have appeared in *Grab-a-Nickel* (Alderson-Broaddus College), *Holler* (Princeton Poetry Project), *Two-Lane Livin' Magazine, The Shine Journal, WestWard Quarterly,* and *The Storyteller.*

Debbie's first book, a chapbook of poetry entitled "Resiliency," was published in November 2012 by *Finishing Line Press* of Georgetown, Kentucky. Her web address is www.debbierichard.com.

Made in the USA
Charleston, SC
23 August 2015